AN ESSAY ON THEOLOGICAL METHOD

Third Edition

AAR

American Academy of Religion
Reflection and Theory in the Study of Religion

Editor
David E. Klemm

Number 05
AN ESSAY ON THEOLOGICAL METHOD
Third Edition
by
Gordon D. Kaufman

AN ESSAY ON THEOLOGICAL METHOD

Third Edition

by
Gordon D. Kaufman

Scholars Press
Atlanta, Georgia

AN ESSAY ON THEOLOGICAL METHOD

Third Edition

by
Gordon D. Kaufman

© 1995
The American Academy of Religion

Library of Congress Cataloging in Publication Data
Kaufman, Gordon D.
    An essay on theological method / by Gordon Kaufman. — 3rd ed.
      p.   cm. — (AAR reflection and theory in the study of religion ;
no. 05)
    ISBN 0-7885-0134-8 (cloth ; alk. paper). —ISBN 0-7885-0135-6
(paper : alk. paper)
    1. Theology—Methodology.   I. Title. II. Series.
BR118.K38   1995
230'.01—dc20   95-20237
                                             CIP

Printed in the United States of America
on acid-free paper

TABLE OF CONTENTS

For my Students—
my teachers

The transcendental idea of a necessary and all-sufficient original being is so overwhelmingly great, so high above everything empirical, the latter being always conditioned, that it leaves us at a loss, partly because we can never find in experience material sufficient to satisfy such a concept, and partly because it is always in the sphere of the conditioned that we carry out our search, seeking there ever vainly for the unconditioned—no law of any empirical synthesis giving us an example of any such unconditioned or providing the least guidance in its pursuit.

Immanuel Kant

Joan. I hear voices telling me what to do. They come from God.
de Baudricourt. They come from your imagination.
Joan. Of course. That is how the messages of God come to us.

G. B. Shaw, *St. Joan*, Scene 1.

What is needed is not the priest of a sentimental aestheticism, nor the prophet of an unimaginative social reform, nor the preacher of a popular uplift, nor even the professor of religion, but the theologian.... For the history of religious thinking makes plain that the role of science and intelligence in religion is not the finding of new and better demonstrations *that* God is, but the continued criticism and purification of *what* God is.

J. H. Randall, Jr.

Preface to the Third Edition

The publication in 1993 of *In Face of Mystery: A Constructive Theology* (Cambridge: Harvard University Press) brought to a culmination the long period of meditation, writing, teaching, and reflection during which I was attempting to work out a full Christian theological stance for today's world on the basis of proposals programmaticly set forth in my *Essay on Theological Method* (1975; second ed., 1979). This earlier work represented my first attempt to present publicly my growing conviction that theology is, and always has been, an activity of what I call the "imaginative construction" of a comprehensive and coherent picture of humanity in the world under God. This way of thinking about theology had emerged gradually in the years I worked on my *Systematic Theology: A Historicist Perspective* (New York: Scribners, 1968), a volume characterized in the Preface as "a work of the theological imagination" (xv). It was largely in reflection on methodological shortcomings of that work—many of them connected with the way in which God and revelation were conceived there (issues widely discussed at that time because of the prominence of the "Death of God" theologies)—that the conception of theological method as essentially a matter of imaginative construction was developed. Discussions with students and others of the first edition of the *Essay* revealed that certain passages could easily give rise to serious misunderstandings; so a second edition, revised to address these matters, was issued in 1979. That version has remained in print up to the present.

Though all my theological teaching and writing since the publication of the *Essay* has been informed by the program it outlined, only now, with the publication of *In Face of Mystery*, has the full range of what was initially envisioned there come clearly into view. In this latter work, however, I have found it necessary to qualify and otherwise alter in some respects what was proposed in the *Essay*. I remain convinced that the understanding of theology presented in that work is fundamentally sound, and its articulation in the second edition is largely adequate in its main contentions. Nevertheless, were I attempting to write such a piece today, I would deal differently with some rather important matters; and I want to call these to the attention of readers.

Chapters 2 and 3 and the Epilogue appear in this new text exactly as found in the second edition, with the exception of a few small changes in wording. More extensive changes, however, were necessary in Chapter 1. The second-edition text of that chapter must seem to most informed readers today to have a somewhat "antique" ring to it, because of its frequent employment of the metaphors of "ground" and "foundation." It is not that a "foundationalist" argument (in the sense of current "anti-foundationalism") is set forth there: a careful reading of the chapter reveals it to be a sustained attack on all supposed "foundations" for theology (Bible, creeds, religious experience, etc.). But use of the metaphor of foundation in the text is not as carefully nuanced as today's discussion requires, and this can easily confuse current readers. For this reason I have replaced many of the foundation metaphors in Chapter 1 with others that should not lead to this sort of misunderstanding, thus (I hope) articulating the argument more clearly. Aside from these very specific changes, the second edition version of this chapter has also been left almost entirely intact.

This does not mean, of course, that Chapter 1, even as now revised, accurately presents my current views in all respects. For example, there is a certain essentialist tone in its rhetoric (as there is throughout the *Essay*): I seem to be making claims about what theology *really is* (namely, God-talk), over against those others who do not realize this or who deliberately take some other position. The very title of Chapter 1, "The Proper Business of Theology," suggests this essentialism. If I were to re-write this chapter (and the rest of the *Essay*) in keeping with my present views, this style of presentation would be eliminated and I would argue—in more pragmatic terms—that a principal advantage gained by defining theology in terms of the problematics of the symbol "God" is that it immediately clears the air of much confusion. Though virtually all theologians employ the word "God" in their work, they often seem to regard it as legitimate to make "theological" judgments and take "theological" positions on many other sorts of issues before (or without) attending to the difficult dialectics of this symbol. Such procedures, however illuminating in some respects, frequently lead into obscurities and confusions that would be averted if theologians took it for granted that in all their work they must take responsibility for coming to terms with the symbol "God."

According to the *Essay* the grammar of the word "God" in most Western literature and reflection is largely of a monotheistic, personalistic, agential sort, ultimately derived from biblical and other related traditions: "God" is generally thought of as referring to the creator of the heavens and the earth, the lord of the universe. It is obvious, of course, that there are many other ways in which the word "God" is employed in English, but my intention in the *Essay* was to bring to light certain methodological issues directly pertinent to the work of Christian (and, in certain respects, Jewish and Muslim) theologians. However, the analysis given there itself shows that it is a mistake to suppose that boundaries of this sort can be drawn tightly: this key word is known and used by all English-language speakers (not only those adhering to these historic faiths), and theological work, therefore, inevitably has a more open and public situatedness and significance than is often realized today. It is not ordinarily acknowledged, moreover, that it is only through the mind's own "imaginative constructive" activities that a symbol with the logical and dialectical peculiarities of "God" (used in a monotheistic sense) can be generated; and that all theological work with this symbol necessarily employs these powers. Central to theological method, therefore, must be the development of (public) practices, disciplines, and criteria in terms of which theologians can order and direct these imaginative constructive powers effectively, as they generate, critically reflect upon, reconstruct, and otherwise employ the symbol "God."

I continue to believe that these basic contentions are correct, but with *In Face of Mystery*—in which I attempted to proceed in terms of the method worked out in the *Essay*—I found it necessary to make some significant alterations and adjustments. The *Essay*, for example, placed considerable emphasis on what was called the proper "order of construction" for methodologically sound theological work (Chapter 3). This order consists of three moments: a moment of phenomenological and scientific description of experience and the world, in which a concept of the world is constructed without regard to the question of whether that concept stands, or can stand, in any intelligible relation to the symbol "God"; the construction of a concept of God that can serve as a relativizing and humanizing focus for the devotion and work of human beings, and which also will significantly relativize the concept of world constructed in Moment I; and the necessary adjustment of these two moments to each other through the imaginative construction of a picture of the world and humanity "under God." In working out the argument of *In Face of Mystery*, however, I found this more or less sequential conception of theological construction to be rather misleading; and I developed instead a more dialectical understanding, with Moments I and III brought into direct interdependence in ways not anticipated (in the *Essay*) to be either possible or appropriate.

The importance of accurate phenomenological and scientific description of humanity and the world (in keeping with the objectives of modern knowledges generally, particularly in the sciences) is still strongly emphasized; but—in accord with my growing pluralistic sensibility—I now found it necessary to acknowledge that a fairly wide variety of religious and/or metaphysical world-pictures could accommodate these data and give them plausible and attractive interpretations. The actual movement toward one or another conception of the world, therefore (Moment I, in the *Essay*), itself turned out to involve elements of faith-commitment as well as concerns about cognitive cogency; and the way in which this was formulated significantly affected the possibility of moving on to construction of a concept of God (the project reserved by the *Essay* to Moment II). When, then, one turned directly to construction of the concept of God itself, one did not really move into a *second* moment of a sequence of three; rather one took up the "climactic moment of a single gradual process within which...a picture of the situation of humanity in the world" was being constructed (*In Face of Mystery*, p. 478, n. 1). In this pattern of theological construction the same three features remain present, but the process of articulating a viable concept of God for today is now conceived throughout as a step-by-step movement of faith and imagination. Although warnings are given in the *Essay* against thinking that its three moments are to be "taken up in simple serial order" (77), the full complexity of their actual dialectical interconnection is not apparent in the text. (I was becoming aware of this late in 1979 after the Second Edition had been published, as can be seen from a brief paper prepared for my students at that time and now published as an Appendix in this book.)

In the *Essay* I identify two paths, regarded as sharply distinct from each other, which theological construction may follow: a "cosmological" approach that emphasizes and builds upon God's relation to the world, and an "existential" approach that focuses largely on the profound human struggles and crises which faith in God is believed to address or overcome (see Chapter 3, nn. 8 and 18). The *Essay* itself is conceived largely in terms of the cosmological approach (as the above summary of the three moments of theological construction suggests), but more existential ways of doing theology are acknowledged as also appropriate and valuable. When the *Essay's* three-moment pattern is loosened up as just proposed, however, and we find ourselves throughout the process of theological construction to be working with humanity-in-the-world—rather than with either the somewhat more objectified "world"-concept of the *Essay* or the strongly individualistic "ego"-concept of more existentialist and pietist perspectives—this contrast of two approaches tends to dissolve away. In *In Face of Mystery* I develop a biohistorical conception of the human which, in its emphasis both on human historicity and on modern ecological and evolutionary understandings of human embeddedness in nature, is intended to overcome precisely the bifurcation between ego-self and world still taken for granted throughout the *Essay* (and particularly visible in the distinction between cosmological and existential theological methods).

This broader and deeper anthropological understanding nullifies yet another deficiency in the *Essay*: virtually no attention is paid to the concrete situatedness of the theologian, as he or she proceeds with the imaginative constructive work of theology. This is a matter the importance of which has become increasingly obvious in recent years, as feminist, African-American, and other "minority" theologians have presented convincing evidence of the extent to which "mainstream" theologies have been shaped by the social locations of the theological guild as a whole and of individual theologians in particular. In our imaginative constructive work today, therefore, it is necessary to take the factor of sociocultural location into account in ways not clearly recognized by traditional theologians or in the *Essay on Theological Method*. (The 1979 modification of the three-moment pattern of theological construction, now printed in the Appendix, gives some attention to this issue with its proposed addition of a Moment Zero to the overall methodological conception.)

Many of today's discussions of the embeddedness of theologians often fail, however, to carry the basic principle which they embody far enough: we need an understanding of theological method that takes seriously not only the social locations of theologians within their own societies, but the historicocultural relativity of Christian and Western traditions generally in the overall context of human religious and cultural history, and the embeddedness of all these matters in the complex processes of life. The biohistorical conception of the human worked out in *In Face of Mystery* is intended to provide an understanding of theologians' contexts that takes into account their sociocultural, historical, and biological dimensions; and the way in which theological construction is developed in that work is intended to reflect this wider and broader view of the human (not yet available to me when I wrote the *Essay*), thus opening up the conception of theological method in important ways. Theology must now be conceived not simply as the imaginative constructive work of individual minds addressing the theological problems they confront: it becomes, rather, a wide-ranging *conversation* among many voices, all involved in imaginative construction but representing significantly diverse standpoints in our thoroughly pluralistic world (see *In Face of Mystery*, esp. Ch. 5).

Our modern/postmodern understanding of human evolutionary and ecological embeddedness in the natural order also makes it difficult to continue thinking in terms of quasi-traditional notions of God (as essentially, e.g., "creator" and "lord" of humanity and the world)— notions with which I worked in my earlier *Systematic Theology* and which were taken too much for granted in writing the *Essay*. It has become clear to me that the metaphors constituting these views require drastic reworking in light of contemporary understandings of the cosmos and of the evolution of life on earth. Accordingly, in *In Face of Mystery* I deconstruct the traditional imagery of the creator/lord/father who performs "mighty acts" in history, and propose instead a reconception in terms of such notions as mystery, serendipitous creativity, the "directional movements" or "trajectories" that have emerged in course of the evolution of the cosmos and the unfolding of human history, and so on (on the one hand); all of these illuminated (for Christian faith) by a reconceived "wider view of Christ" and a reconstructed notion of trinity (on the other hand). The result is a de-reified understanding of God, thoroughly compatible with modern/postmodern understandings of nature and history, but one in which christic images and metaphors still retain normative significance for the ordering of human life. The method of imaginative construction employed in this volume thus leads to conceptions of human being, the world, God, and Christ which, though strikingly different in many ways from those handed down in tradition, nevertheless are continuous with, and are constructed out of materials made available in, Christian (and other Western) traditional and modern resources.

The constructions of God, humanity, the world, and their interrelations presented in *In Face of Mystery* thus depart decisively from the way I understood these matters when the *Essay on Theological Method* was written. Nevertheless, it was because my thinking was informed by the method of imaginative construction sketched in that essay that I was able to develop the more holistic theology of *In Face of Mystery*. It is not to be expected, of course, that others working with methods of imaginative construction will inevitably be led in directions similar to those pursued in that book: this is a methodology that opens and frees the imaginations of theologians to move, in their constructive work, in whatever directions seem to them most persuasive, valuable, meaningful, valid, true. Increasing self-conscious employment of methods of imaginative construction will help widen the ongoing conversation (among those today working in theology) to the full range of issues and problems and points of view with which our pluralized world confronts us. In my view the methodology proposed in the *Essay*—with the qualifications mentioned here—continues to fit well the needs of our time.

G.D.K.
January, 1995

Preface to the Second Edition*

That the contemporary theological scene has become chaotic is evident to everyone who attempts to work in theology. There appears to be no consensus on what the task of theology is or how theology is to be pursued. Some see it as the "science of religion"; others as exposition of the Christian faith; still others as prophetic pronouncement on the conditions of, for example, contemporary American culture (or Western culture generally). There are those who are attempting to develop a "non-sectarian" theology which will not be restricted in meaningfulness to any of the great historic religious traditions; others are attempting to exploit theological insights for developing a more profound understanding of human nature; yet others still see theology as primarily a work of the church attempting to come to better understanding of itself. In all this it usually remains unclear just what is the conception of theology being employed by a particular writer, why he or she calls it *theology* rather than something else, and what methods or procedures are thought properly to characterize this as theological work. It is clear that much hard thinking needs to be addressed to the question of what theology is or can be in this generation, and how it can appropriately proceed.

Of course there has always been disagreement about the methods and objectives of theological work, but the crisis at this time, I think, is more serious than heretofore. It derives from increasing uncertainty about the meaning or status of the *theos* that is supposedly the object of theological analysis and interpretation. Whereas in earlier generations those who called themselves theologians all in some sense "believed in

---

*With the exception of the paragraph added at the end, the text of this Preface is nearly identical to that found in the first edition (1975) of this work.

God" or presupposed the reality of the God about whom they wrote, in our time even this minimal level of agreement cannot be assumed. The central theological problem seems to be, Is it meaningful or useful to speak or think of "God" at all any more? or is talk about God simply a vestige of earlier stages of culture from which we must seek increasingly to free ourselves? Since there is no longer agreement on what the subject-matter of theology is—or even whether it has any distinctive or proper subject-matter of its own—it is little wonder that the field has fallen into chaos, with virtually anyone claiming the title of "theology" for almost anything to which he or she would like to apply it. If theology is to survive as a distinctive and significant form of intellectual activity, it is essential that some order be brought into this confusion and the proper work of theology be clarified.

In the present essay I have attempted to address these issues. I hope that it will prove of use in orienting and guiding future theological work. The essay is divided into three parts. In the first chapter I have sought to analyze and clarify what it is that makes a piece of thinking specifically "theological." The peculiarities of the word "God," I argue, give theology its distinctive character; and the existence of that word in the common language, together with related images and ideas, provides theological reflection with its central problems .

In order to see how theology should proceed, it is necessary, there-fore, to examine the peculiar character and standing of the concept of God. This is undertaken in the second chapter where I attempt to show that much confusion is introduced into theological work by the failure to recognize that the notion of God (like the notion of world) is an imaginative construct built up in quite a different way than the concepts of objects known in and through experience. Theology, therefore, is fundamentally an activity of *construction* (and reconstruction) not of description or exposition, as it has ordinarily been understood in the past; and the failure to grasp this fact has led to mistaken expectations for theology and to the use of misleading criteria both in doing theology and in assessing its conclusions.

How is theological construction actually carried out and how can this activity be rationally analyzed so as to make possible a greater measure of responsible control over it? In the third chapter I have attempted to show that all theological construction involves three moments in complex interrelation with each other, and I have tried to throw some light on the sort of criteria appropriate for constructing and assessing each of these moments.

If the argument of this essay about the constructive character of theology is correct, a far-reaching reorientation of theological work is needed. As such a change is accomplished, theologians should be able to work with greater self-understanding and sophistication and with more promise of success. The view of theology that emerges here is one of a generally significant cultural enterprise with universal and public standards, not a parochial or idiosyncratic activity of interest only to special groups. This conception of the theological task emerged gradually in my mind over a number of years. The breakdown of the neo-orthodox consensus in protestant theology, which had made so much of the authority of "God's revelation" as the ultimate court of appeal, forced me, like others of my generation, to attempt to think through afresh the task of theology and to search for new and more adequate foundations. My teaching and writing in recent years reflects this search. but it has not been until recently that I have felt sufficiently confident about my emerging understanding of theological method to publish it.

The interpretation of theological method set out here is, of course, closely related to my own attempts to do material theology and it could not have been developed apart from that work. Nevertheless, this essay is not intended to be simply a statement of how I do theology. I have attempted here to set out an understanding of what is going on in theological method in the light of that understanding. It is my hope that the position developed here will be of help to theologians of all persuasions, liberal or conservative, Whiteheadian or existentialist or liberationist, Protestant or Catholic or Jewish. No doubt my own understanding of the major doctrines of Christian faith has influenced at important points the conception of theological method expressed in this work—how could it be otherwise?—but I have tried to abstract from such material theological considerations, and I believe the methodological conception to which I have come will prove illuminating for theologians of very different commitments. I hope, therefore, that those who differ with me on such matters will attempt to overlook or forgive the points in this essay at which my material contentions have become overly obtrusive, and will concentrate their attention, rather, on the formal methodological conception I am attempting to set out.

Some may think that such abstraction from material commitments is impossible and absurd, if not blasphemous. How can one develop a valid theological method, a thoughtful Christian may ask, without making specific christological commitments? Is not God's revelation in

Christ the very foundation of the major Christian claims? I must ask a reader who takes a position of this sort to suspend that question as he or she begins this essay. I think it will become clear that theologians of very different persuasions are nevertheless engaged in certain activities that are *formally* quite similar, and these can be analyzed and described. I will attempt to show that this common activity in which theologians are engaged is of general human and cultural significance and that rules and procedures for its proper execution can be to some extent specified. In the course of the essay the role which christological and other specific religious commitments play in theology will be discussed, and at that point the reader is certainly entitled to raise questions and make objections. By then, however, I hope to have persuaded him or her that certain features of theological work are commonly pursued and that it is worthwhile to become self-conscious about these so that they can be tackled with greater insight and care.

Is it necessary to point out that this is an essay on *theology*, not on religion in general or on faith? Religious faith always presupposes (as I shall argue) certain theological constructions, and it may also give rise to reflective and analytic activity on the basis of which criticism and further construction must be attempted. But faith is primarily an attitude of devotion to or trust in God, or in some other reality deemed appropriate; it is the basic stance of a self or community, a "form of life" (Wittgenstein). Theology, however, is not so much devotion to the symbols of faith as the attempt to *understand* those symbols and the way they function in human life, to criticize and reinterpret them so they will more adequately achieve their purpose, and finally (as I am especially emphasizing in this essay) to reconstruct them, sometimes radically. Theology thus, like faith, arises out of response to religious symbols and their meaning, but instead of expressing itself in simple trust or devotion it is particularly sensitive to difficulties or problems in the formulation and implications of those symbols. It is a *deliberate human activity* directed toward criticizing and reconstructing the symbols by which faith lives and to which faith responds. If faith is a gift of God, as it has been traditionally understood, theology is clearly human work, and we must take full responsibility for it. But it is human work that emerges out of faith's own need for more adequate orientation and symbolization. Such theological activity may reinforce—or it may weaken further—the religious stance.

Whether the religiously devout will want to engage themselves much in theology is perhaps a question to be seriously faced. Theological questioning has shaken the foundations of more than one person's faith. However, theological problems implicit in faith and its symbolism cannot always be easily avoided. In our own time, for example, the women's liberation movement has called attention to the prejudicial implications of the fact that the fundamental symbolism of Christianity and Judaism is almost totally male-oriented.[1] In consequence many women—and also some men—have found it increasingly difficult to use these symbols either in worship or in self-understanding. But if God can no longer be understood as "Father" or "Lord," can no longer even be referred to as "he," what is to become of faith oriented fundamentally in terms of these symbols? Must it die? Can it move to new and more adequate forms of symbolization? Is faith without any specific symbolization a possible way out? These are all theological problems, but they have emerged suddenly in a contemporary crisis in religious faith. I hope that the understanding of theology set out in the present essay will make issues of this sort more intelligible and, even more, that it will suggest how they are to be met.

The almost exclusive use of male symbolism in Western religious and theological language has posed difficult problems in the writing of this essay. I have tried throughout to avoid using the term "man" in its generic sense, as referring to both men and women, or the pronoun "he" in a similarly inclusive sense—though this has not been without stylistic cost—for I am persuaded that our traditional linguistic practice in these matters expresses and perpetuates conceptions of male superiority which, now that we are aware of this, can no longer be tolerated. There are similar problems, of course, connected with speaking of God as "he" or "him." In my opinion, however, no satisfactory substitute for the use of these pronouns has yet been devised— certainly "it" will not do, and "he/she" is cumbersome and awkward, as is the attempt to avoid the use of pronouns altogether. Hence, with considerable misgivings I have retained in these pages the use of "he" and its variants to refer to God, though I recognize their inadequacies and hope my readers will do so as well. I wish strongly to repudiate the view that questions of gender are in any way relevant to a properly constructed concept of God. For my growing awareness of the significance of this issue, I must thank the emerging group of women theologians, including especially some of my own students.

My students must be thanked, also, for help at many points with the major contentions of this essay: early versions of the ideas in it were explored from time to time in seminars and classes, and preliminary drafts, and subsequently the first edition, have been used in seminars on theological method. I have benefited immensely from the resulting student comment and criticism.

Messrs. Stephen Dunning, my former teaching assistant and colleague, David Pacini and Joseph Runzo should be singled out for special mention in this connection. A number of former students, now colleagues teaching in various institutions, also took the time to read an early draft of this essay and to comment upon it: Professor Wayne Proudfoot of Columbia University, Professor Carl Raschke of the University of Denver, Professor George Rupp of Harvard Divinity School, and Professor Mark Taylor of Williams College. A preliminary version of the second chapter was presented for criticism and comment to two theological discussion groups of which I am a member; and my long time friend and colleague, Professor Van A. Harvey, now of Stanford University, also gave me the benefit of his criticism. The responses received from these various readers have saved me from numerous infelicities of expression as well as some outright errors.

Finally, for another kind of indispensable help, I must thank Mrs. Ruth Kooman and Mrs. Christine Langlais, who faithfully typed and re-typed version after version of these pages.

I am grateful to all these, named and unnamed, for their assistance.

૪

The main emphases of this second edition of my *Essay on Theological Method* remain the same as in the first edition, and much of the text is identical. The first edition, however, stressed too much the distinction of theological reflection and analysis from worship and religious experience, thus rendering very obscure the experiential grounding of and motivation for theological work. I have tried to repair this major defect in the present edition and, in addition, have made a number of other improvements in and amplifications of the text. I am grateful to students and others who have helped me to see more clearly these issues and how they should be addressed.

G.D.K.
June, 1978

---

[1]For a full discussion of these issues see (along with many others now appearing) Mary Daly, *Beyond God the Father* (Boston: Beacon Press, 1973). Other groups also, e.g., black theologians and "third world" theologians, have increasingly been pointing out ways in which the dominant theologies have been biased and ideological, and this raises significant religious as well as theological issues. Unfortunately, I will not be able to discuss any of this literature within the bounds of this essay since my intention is not to survey the contemporary scene but rather to develop a constructive position on the task and procedures of theology. I believe the position I have developed here does take account of, and help to make comprehensible, the claims of these recent critics of the theological establishment. More important, it provides a conception of theology which should be of help, I think, as they attempt to develop constructive theological positions of their own.

1

The Proper Business of Theology

"To whom will you liken me and make me equal, and compare me, that we may be alike?... I am the first and I am the last; besides me there is no god."

Isaiah 46:5; 44:6

What is the proper subject-matter and task of theology? What problems are its peculiar concern, and how are they to be addressed? What is it that makes an essay or a book "theological," as distinguished, say, from "psychological" or "ethical" or "political"? These questions are not often addressed in the current scene, even in what purports to be theological literature. Instead, we are presented with many different "theologies" issuing from a variety of cultural or psychological positions or problems—a "theology of play," a "theology of hope," a "theology of revolution," a "theology of experience," "biblical theology," "black theology," "women's liberation theology," and the like. The assumption seems to be that theology is written whenever one takes up a problem or attitude or interest and attempts to probe its "deeper" meanings and implications with the help of certain so-called religious or theological terms and perspectives.

There is some justification for this somewhat casual approach to the question of the nature and methods of theology. To the extent that theology attempts to deal with matters of "ultimate concern" (Tillich), it would seem justifiable to begin theological work with virtually any "preliminary concern" and then attempt to move through and beneath it to that which underlies and expresses itself there as the final or lasting or ultimate. Or, to put the same point in more traditional theological language, if it is God, the Creator of all things both visible and invisible, about whom we are attempting to speak in theology, any single point in the created order ought to be as valid as any other for a point of departure for theological talk. There is no position which cannot be a starting-point for theological reflection: the issue is not where one begins, but how one makes the movement from the preliminary to the ultimate, from creatures to God.[1]

I

The question about how that movement is or can be made has often been short-circuited in Christian theological reflection by the claim that theology is rooted in and founded upon God's revelation, vouchsafed to humankind in the biblical witness or in authoritative church pronouncement. From this point of view it is held that theology must and does begin with biblical statement or church dogma, that the theologian's business is analysis and interpretation of what is made available in these authoritative propositions or documents. The materials with which theology works are thus clearly given and need not themselves be defended or justified. Indeed, it might be held (Barth) that all attempts at such justification involve serious misunder-standings of the theological enterprise, for they suggest both that God's revelation requires some kind of human certification before it can be accepted, and that is blasphemy; and that there is some way of humanly establishing or proving what only God could be in a position to certify, and that is absurd. Hence, the theologian must work with what has been given—given by God, of course—and proceed to explicate and interpret that. In this sense, it may be held, theology always presupposes a certain faith, namely the faith that God has in fact revealed himself; and this faith is not itself subject to theological questioning or doubt. Theology is thus a work of the church and for the church; it is an analysis and interpretation of the faith of those who already stand within the "theological circle" (Tillich).

As an interpretation of the defining moves of theological work, such a view is very misleading, for it presupposes as self-evident and clear and already given concepts that surely must be established and explained. In saying that we are to begin with "God's revelation," it is assumed that we know what we are talking about when we say "God" and "revelation," and that there is nothing problematical about these terms. But of course that begs some important questions: What do we (i.e., us human beings) mean when we say "God"? How does one undertake, within the created order, to speak of him? What validity has our concept of God? What is its proper use? And what of the concept of revelation? How is it to be understood? To deal with such issues it will not do to presuppose the very concepts in question by talking about "God's revelation" as if these concepts were just givens to be taken for granted. Like any others, these concepts have been created and developed in and through human processes of reflection on life and interpretation of experience. It is only because some persons at certain times and places found it useful and meaningful and perhaps even necessary to speak of "God's revelation," in order to make sense of the life and history which they were undergoing, that these terms and concepts were developed and employed within the human sphere at all. And it is of course only because such concepts were developed in the past that we have them available now (within the church or without it) for our use as theologians. Theology may not simply presuppose these concepts and then proceed to employ them in more or less traditional ways. The question about the moves that lead into theology is closely connected with the question about how and why such concepts were created and shaped in the first place, and how they can be sustained and reconstructed now. It is a much broader and deeper question than the theological positivism of much of the Christian tradition has supposed.

The point that I am arguing here may be made in another more sociological way. To suppose that theology is essentially a work of the church[2] and that therefore theologians can or must accept without question the "faith" of the church (as found in scripture or dogma) is to proceed on too simple-minded a view of the way in which the church's life is imbedded within the society and culture in which it is found. It ignores the fact, for example, that the entire vocabulary of the church—including such central terms as God, man, church, reconciliation, revelation, prayer, faith—consists of ordinary words from the everyday language of people. Everyone who speaks English (or German or Russian or Italian, in the corresponding cases) knows and understands these words and uses them in appropriate situations. Their meaning, thus, is tied to the life of the culture as a whole and can be grasped only in connection with that broad cultural base and experience: it is by no means the private property of the church or of those who are members of the church. Doubtless, the life of the churches, and the peculiar history and experience of the churches, have contributed to that meaning; but that life and history are not its exclusive ground. To attempt to understand theological terms and concepts, then, only by reference to life in the church is obviously arbitrary and can only result in truncated and one-sided interpretations. As we shall see later, there is a place for special reference to particular traditions of meaning and special communities of interpretation, but this is obviously not the place where theological reflection actually begins. Theological terms and concepts are rooted in the wide experience and history of a whole culture, or a mixture of cultures, and until we discern the way in which theological reflection is grounded upon and built up out of this broader cultural experience, we will misunderstand it.

I am not holding that it is false to claim that theology in some sense—indeed, in a theologically very important sense—may be grounded on "God's revelation." I am holding that it is a mistake to suppose that that claim tells us how to begin our theological work, i.e., that it tells us where we as theologians, as human thinkers, can or should turn to do theology. Theology is and always has been a human work: it emerges out of and interprets human historical events and experiences; it utilizes humanly created and shaped terms and concepts; it is carried out by human processes of meditation, reflection, ratiocination, speaking, writing and reading. We as theologians can perform only these human activities; we cannot in any way do God's speaking, acting, inspiring or providential guiding. Our theological work has to be understood, therefore, entirely in terms of what *we* can do on the basis of what is available to us. If in the course of that work we conclude that God also has been involved in it and with it, making himself known in and through human experience and revealing himself through particular historical sequences—and that therefore the ultimate foundation of theological work is God's self-revelatory activity—that will be a highly significant conclusion. But it is important to note that this claim about God's guidance and revelation will be a conclusion not an opening premise; it emerges out of significant prior experience, reflection and reasoning, and these roots must be uncovered and made clear if we are to come to genuine understanding of what we are doing when we are theologizing.

It might be useful here to put the matter in terms of the common distinction between the "order of being" and the "order of knowing." If we conclude that God is properly conceived as the Creator of all other being, the source and ground of all that is, then it will be correct to regard him as the ultimate source of human faith and of the theological attempts to understand faith and its object. This is how the order of being will have to be conceived theologically. But this is certainly not the order in which we come to know God, ourselves and other beings, or the order in which we can do theology. The order of knowing with respect to God will have to be uncovered psychologically and epistemologically; and it may not correspond at all to the order of being, since it is affected so profoundly by the capacities of our cognitive apparatus. We must find the point at which human theological reflection can and does begin, and then we must trace the course through which it passes as it develops. It is a confusion of this order in which we come to know with the order of being that has led theologians to suppose that they must, or even can, begin with God or with God's revelation in their theological exposition. Our concern here must initially be with the path that culminates in such speech about God and his revelation. That path will necessarily fall somewhere in the speech or experience or history prior to this sort of technical theological talk.

II

It may be supposed that theological language is largely grounded upon and develops directly out of "religious experience." This view is an expression of the notion that all our language and thought is rooted in experience and is essentially the articulation and interpretation of experience. To understand theological language, then, we must locate and describe that particular domain of human experience, or those special qualities of experience, which it is grounded upon and expresses. Careful phenomenological study should be able to uncover this pretheological basis of theology. We should thus come into a position to see how theological terms and concepts are created and shaped; and we should be able to develop criteria for assessing the adequacy of those notions we have inherited from the tradition, criteria that will also assist us in reformulating and reconstructing them to serve more adequately in the contemporary situation. Thus a whole theological program can be developed on the premise that theology is to be understood as essentially the interpretation of religious experience.[3]

An initial problem that confronts this approach is the difficulty of determining just what is to be understood as "religious experience." Is it to be thought of as the experience of a special religious object—the holy, the infinite, God? Or is it a special quality of experience, the sense of "absolute dependence," a sense of oneness with the universe, the experience of exaltation or insight, or of anxiety or guilt? All of these and more have been claimed as the central religious experience(s), and it is not clear on just what basis one decides among the competitors. Certainly it is not possible to maintain that all these terms really mean the same thing or refer to the same experience. Which one(s) more adequately or exactly refer us to the raw preconceptual bases of theology? An argument could be made for almost any of these (and has been) as well as for many other possibilities (transcendence, the absolute, power, the unconditional, the ultimate). All seem to have a certain religious quality or significance and thus to be appropriate candidates; none stands out as clearly primary.

The difficulty here arises from framing our questions in terms of an oversimple conception of the relation between individual experience and its social context of language, custom and institutions. A three-stage model seems to be presupposed. First, there is the raw experience of the individual as the foundation of all speaking, thinking and acting. Second, the individual reflects upon or thinks about this experience. And third, he or she may finally choose to communicate that experience and reflection to other persons through language, participate in a ritual, or take up a role in an institution. We have here a picture of the completely private self living out and experiencing its life, with language and other forms of social interaction indispensable only at the third stage of communication; although these might have some uses and importance at the stage of meditation and reflection, they seem to have no effect or significance at all at the primary level of experiencing.

I cannot here set out a full theory of the social basis of all individual experience,[4] but it is necessary at least to indicate something of the importance of language. Language is at work at all three of these levels of experience. There is no such thing as a raw pre-linguistic experience of "transcendence," say, as distinguished from the experience of "ultimacy" or of the "infinite." Each of these "experiences" is shaped, delimited and informed by the linguistic symbols which also name it. Without those symbols to guide our consciousness these "experiences" would not be available to us at all. Moreover, these symbols are not bare and empty names for the experiences which they supposedly designate. They carry nuances of meaning derived from their various uses in the language and their connections with other terms. "Ultimacy" refers to that which is last or final, and it gains its meaning not simply by naming some religious quality in experience but through its connections with the final terms in various sorts of series, and with many kinds of experience of completion or ending. "Infinite" does not refer in the first instance to a peculiar isolated and unique reality, incomparable with any other, but is a negative term meaning simply "not finite," without limits or restrictions; it gets its meaning (at least in large part) through our ideas and experiences of limitations and boundaries of many different sorts and our power to imagine what it would be like if this or that restriction—or every restriction were removed. "Transcendence" is a spatial metaphor which refers literally to the fact or act of surmounting or climbing over or ascending; it has only gradually come to acquire the further meanings of surpassing, excelling, and the like. Though we might at times speak of the "experience of transcendence" or of the "sense of ultimacy," these are by no means simple pre-cognitive, pre-linguistic experiences. They are highly complex modes of consciousness which would be of a quite different sort were they formed and informed by different linguistic symbols.

Our "religious experience," whatever this turns out to be, is not raw, pre-conceptual, and pre-linguistic, the undialectical foundation on which theology can be built. Like all the rest of experience, it is always a construction or composite, heavily dependent for its form and qualities on the learned terms and concepts which give it particular flavor and shape.[5] The language in which we think, the traditions we have inherited, articulate certain connections between concepts and certain relations between words and ideas; and it is in terms of these connections and valuations and interpretations that we focus our attention in experience, divide it up the way we do, and see in it what we can. It is, thus, the availability in our language of words like "infinite," "holy," and "God" that gives our experience in its "religious" aspects its peculiar quality and shape.

It would be truer to say that the language we speak provides a principal foundation for our religious experience than to hold that some pre-conceptual, pre-linguistic raw experience is the principal foundation of our theological language and thought. The basic meaning of these so-called religious terms is not so much derived from raw experience as it is given with and in the language and images we have learned from childhood. Grasping their meanings does not involve so much the question of what experiences one has had as how these words are used in English. It is an issue to be explored by etymological and lexicographical research (what Wittgenstein called grammatical study), assuming that we understand such researches to include broad philosophical and theological investigations into the meaning and use of words. Only on the basis of historical study—including, of course, studies of and "feel for" contemporary usage—of the meaning and use of such terms as "infinite," "transcendence," and "God," can we decide what these words can properly be taken to mean and how they are related and interrelated with each other. All the terms and images we have been discussing here, together with others like "light," "joy," "peace" and "salvation," are related or connected in a configuration that articulates—for English speakers—what they call "religious experience." What the structure of that configuration—and hence of that experience—is, cannot be grasped apart from attending to the uses of these terms in the language.

Western theology should be seen first of all, thus, as a part of the language and traditions which have shaped Western experience. Given different linguistic traditions and histories, religious experience in the West, and theology as well, would be quite different. Or, to say the same thing from the other side, reflection on experience and life in other cultures (which have been shaped by other linguistic developments and traditions) uses different categories and focuses on different emphases and values. And experience itself in those other cultures, shaped as it is by those languages and complexes of images and conceptual structures, is of a quite different sort, with different qualities, values, emphases, meanings. It should not surprise us, then, to find that the peculiar kind of intellectual activity that we call "theology," with its focus on the concept of "God" and its elaborate doctrinal development, is not universally found in all cultures and religious traditions but is especially characteristic of Western Christian history. Other cultures have developed in different ways, and their traditions of intellectual reflection have likewise moved down quite different paths.[6]

The upshot of our brief exploration of religious experience as the basis of theological work has been somewhat negative. I am not seeking here to deny that there is such a thing as religious experience, nor do I wish to deny its importance for human life. I do want to claim that it does not provide the principal basis for or entry into theological work. As we have seen, what religious experience is in any particular case is itself determined by the images and the linguistic and conceptual categories available in the tradition of the experiencer. These shape and form and define the experience and interpret its meaning to him or her. The raw pre-conceptual and pre-linguistic ground of religious experience is simply not available to us for direct exploration, description or interpretation, and therefore it cannot provide us with a starting-point for theological work. This is provided, rather, by tradition and language, and it is to them that we must look in order to proceed .

This does not mean, however, that theological work can be carried on without reference to experience or that experience is irrelevant to it. Categories and concepts have no meaning or function except as they shape and interpret experience. Apart from experience, unfilled with experience, they are empty and useless. That many traditional concepts and categories—including especially "God"—no longer seem related to our actual experience but seem to float free, as more or less empty forms with little contemporary meaning or use, has today become a major theological problem. It may be that these ways of forming experience and interpreting it are dying out. This is part of what is meant by those who say that we are moving into a wholly "secular" or "post-Christian" age. Concepts (or images) like "God," "Christ," "church," "salvation," "sacraments," "heaven," "hell"—also "theology"—in terms of which experience and life were appropriated and understood for centuries, now no longer seem really functional in many quarters. Others—psychological, aesthetic, political—have taken their places; experience has come to have different shapes, flavors, meanings. Whether these claims are true or not, I do not wish to argue here. My point is that to say theology is concerned largely with certain categories and concepts and traditions, and that the analysis of these must provide the starting-point for theology, is not to say that experience is unimportant or is to be neglected. For all our categories and concepts have been created in the efforts of men and women to grasp and comprehend their developing experience, and they have meaning only so far as they succeed in forming and interpreting experience. Their ability to deal with experience—including especially experience of the new, the unexpected, the startling—is thus the ultimate test of their viability and significance.

In this sense, as the ultimate test of our terms and ideas, experience is the final court of appeal for all theological work. Experience thus has the *last* word with theology but not the *first* word: theological reflection must be directed initially toward the central terms and concepts and images provided by tradition and history. Experience will sit in judgment on that tradition and history to see whether these can still make sense of our lives.

III

It may appear that our argument has brought us back to the position we rejected a moment ago, that theology is grounded upon acceptance of the authority of scripture or church pronouncement. But that is not the case. In saying that theological reflection must be rooted in categories and concepts and images provided by tradition and history, I am neither claiming that theology begins by invoking authority nor am I restricting the scope of theological inquiry to specific documents or dogmas accorded special significance in the churches. The language of the churches and of scripture, as we have seen, including their so-called religious or theological terms, is common language in the societies and cultures where church and scripture are found. It is this common language and these ordinary uses that theology always presupposes, and with which, therefore, it should begin, not with special or technical meanings alleged to be authoritative because "revealed" by God. All special and technical meanings are variations or developments of the ordinary language, building upon it, refining it, transforming it. They are thus parasitic upon it and cannot be understood apart from it, and for this reason it is delusory to suppose we have reached the foundations of theology when we turn to them.

Theology, thus, works largely with public, not private or parochial, materials. It is not restricted either to the language and traditions of a particular esoteric community (the church) or to the peculiar experience of unusual individuals. Everyone speaks the common language; everyone knows, understands and uses (to some degree) the words with which theology begins and which it analyzes. Hence, there is no problem of how one can get into some charmed "circle of faith" or "theological circle" in order to do theology or to understand what is going on in theology. We are already there simply by virtue of speaking and understanding English. Theology need be no more parochial or exclusive than any other discipline.[7]

How does this ordinary speech become specifically *theology?* Two delimiting moves are involved: a) Theology does not attempt to deal with the entire language and its imagery but attends to certain key terms or complexes of terms, such words as "holy," "divine," "sacred," "transcendent" and the like, and focused particularly, or "presided over" (I. T. Ramsey), by "God."[8] b) Theology does not consist merely in speaking or understanding these words but rather in reflection upon them, criticism and interpretation of them, and deliberate extension, refinement or reconstruction of their meaning and use. Theology is the disciplined effort to see what we are trying to do and say with these complexes of meaning so as to enable us to say and do them better— more accurately, more precisely, more effectively. In this sense, as Ludwig Wittgenstein has put it, "Theology [is] grammar."[9] As with all grammar, it involves the attempt to determine not only how the language is actually used by its speakers and writers, but also the rules governing that use, so that it will become possible to distinguish proper from improper use, clear and adequate from misleading and confusing forms of expression. This prescriptive dimension of grammar—always founded upon and emergent out of a sense for, and descriptive studies of, usage—enables it to help shape language into a vehicle which expresses our intentions with greater precision, thus facilitating a fuller and clearer consciousness of those intentions. Theology also, as grammar, not only attempts to describe how men and women in fact talk about God; it searches out the rules governing the use of such talk so that it will be possible to see more clearly just what that talk is intending to express. Thus, theological analysis aims to distinguish better from worse forms of expression and seeks to define adequate or proper speech about God. I shall say more later about how this is done;

for now, I am simply trying to delimit the special area which can properly be called theology and the particular form of activity that is carried on there.

It is not possible in this essay, nor would it be appropriate, to make a full-scale study of the theological vocabulary in order to ascertain what terms fall into it, how they are used, and how they are related to each other; that is a project for historical, phenomenological and linguistic studies on the one hand, and systematic theology, on the other.[10] It is necessary, however, for us to examine that central and most problematic theological term, "God." Theology *(theos-logos)* is "words" or "speech" about God—"God-talk." All the other terms of the theological vocabulary in one way or another qualify, explain or interpret what is meant by "God," or indicate ways in which God is related to or involved in human experience and the human world. In this sense they are all derivative from or secondary to "God." It should not be supposed, however, that this means they can be logically deduced from the concept of God and that the only real theological problem, therefore, is to get that concept straight. That would be an overly simple and too undialectical way of understanding the matter. For words and concepts are not self-enclosed things which simply are what they are: they interpenetrate each other in many complex ways, qualifying and conditioning each other reciprocally. So the secondary and tertiary terms of the theological vocabulary, precisely through their explanation and interpretation of the primary term "God," expand, delimit and qualify its meaning in important respects. The theological vocabulary is an organic whole and must be studied as such. Though God himself may be conceived as radically independent, underived, self-contained reality—as alone having "aseity"—with all other reality derivative, secondary and contingent, the *concept* of God cannot properly be understood to have that exalted status: it is shaped and affected by many considerations and must be qualified, defined and redefined in very careful and complex ways if it is to be properly constructed. Far from being an independent given from which all other concepts can be deduced, it is the most complex and difficult of all concepts, in some ways dependent on and conditioned by all others. (Our understanding of what it means to speak of "the Creator of all things visible and invisible" will be necessarily and decisively affected by what we take all those visible and invisible things to be; and as our conception of the created order changes, our conception of the Creator will also necessarily change in corresponding ways.) However central and fundamental to the theological enterprise is the concept (or image) of God, therefore, it cannot be dealt with independently or in isolation from the rest of the theological vocabulary. It gains its meaning precisely through its connections with other terms and ultimately thus with the whole of human experience.

Nonetheless it is possible, and quite important in this context, to focus attention on certain logical peculiarities of the (use of the) word "God." How is it that this word can serve as a focus for organizing a whole vocabulary? What kind of meaning or use does that vocabulary give to this word when thus focused by it? To bring clearly into view certain issues involved in these questions, we shall have to explore the peculiar (logical or grammatical) character and function of the word "God."[11]

Whether the *doctrine* of God is explicitly developed in an essay or book, an implicit concept of God must be present if the work is properly to be regarded as *theo*logical. If there is no evident way of moving from what is explicitly discussed to talk about God, there is no reason to designate the essay as "theological" at all, as contrasted with, say, a "psychological," or "sociological," or "literary," or perhaps even a "religious" essay.[12] But this means that in order to do theology properly one must have a fairly clear idea of what talk about God involves so that the way in which the idea of God functions can be kept in mind as one attends to the actual subject-matter which he or she is investigating. A great deal of confusion and superficiality in current theological literature might have been avoided if this rule had been kept in view. However, since the concept of God has become so difficult and problematical in our time, would-be theologians often choose simply to put it out of mind for a time while they write on any number of other topics of current interest, all the while claiming to be doing theology. With such methodological laziness it should surprise no one that much of what passes for theology today is very unconvincing.

IV

The word "God" has been used in many different ways in Western literature, and I cannot begin to explore all the alternatives here. There are polytheistic uses and monotheistic uses, widely influential mythopoeic pictures and highly idiosyncratic philosophical conceptions, metaphysical notions of transcendence or infinity and religious images of a heavenly father or divine judge. There are views that emphasize God's absoluteness and oneness as the Source of all that is, and others that see God as but one of several powers that constitute the world. Some worship God as the Holy One beyond good and evil; others acclaim him as the utterly righteous One in whom all morality is grounded. Obviously there are many ways to view God, and each no doubt can be given some significant justification. Moreover, if the argument to be worked out in the present essay is correct, all these conceptions of God are human constructs, and the problem of developing criteria for choosing among them is among the most difficult and urgent facing contemporary theology. It would be highly improper, therefore, to demand full agreement from readers on the following attempt to say something about what the word "God" means in typical Western usage.

Some provisional characterization of God must be suggested here, however, if we are to grasp the special peculiarities and difficulties of the problems with which theology must deal. This need not be an entirely arbitrary exercise: despite all the diversity in Western talk about God, certain broadly monotheistic lines can be discriminated, I think, on which there would be wide, though by no means unanimous, agreement. Making these explicit will give us a point of reference for clarifying the peculiar nature and tasks of theology. (I trust it goes without saying that I am not attempting here to impose my notion of God on readers for whom the following characterization seems seriously misleading; I would hope that such readers could make the necessary transpositions and adjustments so that the analysis and interpretation of theological method which follows would prove illuminating and helpful to them.)

I would like to suggest that with the word "God" we are attempting to indicate the last or ultimate point of reference to which all action, consciousness and reflection can lead. No regressive reflection seeking to push back to an ultimate starting-point, no creative action moving toward an unstructured future, no appreciative feeling of worship or devotion expressing the orientation of the whole life of the self can intend some reality "beyond" God. This is what is meant by calling God the "First Cause" or "Creator": he is the ground and foundation of everything that is, and there can be nothing behind or beyond him which in any way founds or grounds anything in us or in our world. This is expressed also by the claim that God alone is holy, the only one worthy of the full devotion and worship of every person. Again, it is expressed in the acclamation of God as the Alpha and Omega, the first and the last, the one "from [whom] and through [whom] and to [whom] are all things" (Rom 11:36). This does not mean, of course, that *empirically* God is the beginning and end of everything that is, as though this were something we could observe. Rather, this is a *conceptual* matter: the idea of "God" is the idea of that absolute beginning and ending point beyond which it is never possible to push. Many different titles have been used to express this in the tradition: God is said to be "absolute," "unconditioned," "infinite," "necessary being," "perfect being" and so forth. Perhaps the best succinct characterization that makes this point is that of Anselm: God is that "than which nothing greater can be conceived."[13]

This idea of an ultimate reference point (whether conceived as "God" or in some other way) is no optional or dispensable one. All experience involves a unification of plurality and thus presupposes (at least implicitly) some ultimate unifying ground. In primal cultures and in unreflective persons the questions of how experience and the world can have this unity, and what it is that grounds it, do not come to expression; but with increasing reflection upon experience and life, and the deliberate attempt to order and understand them, some ultimate point of reference in terms of which all else is understood must be proposed. It need not be a singular being such as "God" or "the One"; in polytheism, for example, it is a structure or order, the fate which lies behind both gods and humans and to which they are subordinate, that provides the point of reference for interpreting all that happens and all that is. In the Hebraic world reflection on experience and on the polytheistic mythologies which interpreted it brought forth the conception of God (Yahweh) as the one transcendent point to which all could be referred and which relativizes all else. "Hear, O Israel: The Lord our God, the Lord is one; and you shall love the Lord your God with all your heart, and with all your soul, and with all your might" (Deut 6:4–5). Further reflection on this "radical monotheism"[14] in the cultures heir to ancient Israel has greatly refined the idea and made clear its peculiar logical character, to which we must now attend.

In order to function as an ultimate point of reference, God cannot be conceived as simply one more of the items of ordinary experience or knowledge, in some way side by side with the others; he must be thought of as "beyond" all the others, not restricted or limited by any of them but himself relativizing all. If he did not have this unique logical status, he could not be regarded as the ground of the unity of everything experienced but would himself be a part of that which had to be unified. It is this logical point that notions of God's absoluteness or unconditionedness attempt to make. Because God has the special logical standing suggested by these conceptions, he is able to meet the fundamental religious need for an ultimate ground of security in the face of such human crises as death, natural catastrophe or military conquest. The concept of God is related to experience, then, not as indicating one more item experienced but as referring to the ground of its unity. Since God functions this way in monotheism, it is possible to make a radical distinction between God and all idols—all merely finite realities mistaken for God—and God can thus perform the immensely important religious task of unmasking the idols. Only in monotheism can and does God function in this way rather than simply as one of the many powers to which we are subjected.

In a radical and consistent monotheism the idea of God is very peculiar, indeed unique. God cannot properly be conceived (as so often in popular religion) as one more object like all others, only somewhat larger. He cannot be thought of as like one of those many things of which we can ask rather simply, Does it exist? and then can devise rather straightforward procedures for finding the answer. Rather, the concept of God functions as a *limiting idea*, as the idea of that beyond which we cannot go either in experience, thought or imagination. Unlike the concept of any ordinary object, which is the idea of something that can be readily observed and can be examined in various ways, a limiting idea is of that which can only be approached but never actually reached, certainly not surpassed. The question of the existence or status of that which limits all experience is thus very different from the question of the existence or status of one of the ordinary objects of experience. Moreover, in the case of "God" we are not just speaking of a limit of experience; we are speaking of the *absolute limit*, the limit of all limits, "limit" raised to a second power. We are attempting to speak of that in terms of which all else is to be understood, which therefore so transcends everything else that it cannot be understood as gaining its meaning or being by reference to it. This does not mean that God is *experienced* as somehow isolated from everything else or that he is known by anyone without reference to knowledge of anything else. Rather, once again, this is a *conceptual* matter: the *idea* of God is the idea of that on which all else depends but itself depends on nothing else; it is the idea of absolute aseity. From whence this idea comes we shall have to explore later, but it is certainly not gained directly or immediately from experience as our ideas of ordinary objects may seem to be.

The term "God," then, is typically taken to stand for or name the ultimate point of reference or orientation for all life, action, devotion, reflection. I have been expressing this matter abstractly here, trying to bring out the peculiar logical character of the idea. In actual religious life and experience all this is usually expressed much more concretely in images which speak more directly to the existential needs of finite beings: God is spoken of as "our Father in heaven"; as our "Lord" or "King" to whom all devotion is due; as the "Creator of the heavens and the earth," "the Maker of all things visible and invisible"; as the "Judge of all the earth" who will effect a final separation of the good from the bad, the righteous from the wicked, the wheat from the chaff; as our "Savior," the "good Shepherd," who leads us "through the valley of the shadow of death" to our ultimate destination where "goodness and mercy" shall be our portion "forever." Actual human speech about God, thus, is not abstract logical talk about an "ultimate limit" but rather talk about life and the world, about our deepest problems, about catastrophe and triumph, about human misery and human glory. It is about what is really important in life, how we are to live, how comport ourselves, which styles of life are genuinely human and which dehumanizing. But it is and can be talk about these matters only because it claims to be about that ultimate point of orientation to which all else must be referred. It is because the idea of God has the peculiar logical character which I have been sketching that the images in which it is often expressed can have the religious and experiential significance which they do.

Of course human existence and the world can be seen in other ways than as being under God, being God's creation. That is, the ultimate point of reference, the ultimate limiting idea, need not be conceived as "God." One can take the foundation of all else to be, for example, *matter*. Life, then, will be seen as a highly complex form of matter, and human life—the product of a long evolutionary process—will also be seen as essentially a complexification of what is fundamentally material reality; on such a view all existence, life and meaning would have to be interpreted in basically materialistic terms. Reality can also be seen in terms of sheer animal vitality, as will, striving, will-to power; and an interpretation of human existence and its meaning can be given in these terms. Or it can be grasped as rational order or as a battleground between the forces of light and the forces of darkness, as the playground of the gods or as the outworking of karma or of inscrutable fate. Doubtless there are many other ways. Each of these intuitions of, or claims about, the real provides the basis for a mythology or world-picture in terms of which all experience can be grasped and all life ordered. Sometimes attempts are made to analyze carefully and articulate precisely the structure of such a view of the world and of humanity within it; the result is what is called "metaphysics."

In Western culture, however, the reality in which all life and meaning is grounded has most frequently been understood as *God*; indeed, one could argue that in investigating the meaning of "God," theology is exploring the principal orientation which has shaped the West. It has been largely in connection with the notion of God—and analysis of the meaning of that notion—that the idea of a single ultimate point of reference was developed; and in some writers the idea of God has been taken to have just this formal meaning and nothing more. Many philosophers, for example, have felt entitled to use the word "God" to name what they regarded as the highest or the deepest or the most fundamental, even though some features of their conception of reality were at variance with what otherwise might seem implied by that term. But the word "God" does not bear only this highly formal meaning; it also carries important material connotations, and these have been emphasized particularly in the religious uses to which it has been put. Here "God" ordinarily designates not merely the ultimate point of reference, but *a particular way of construing that point*, namely, as personal or agential in character: the notion of God in its material aspects has been based largely on the model of the human person or agent.[15] Since many philosophers (and some theologians) have ignored or rejected these material dimensions of meaning (which they regarded as misleading anthropomorphisms) when working out their metaphysical positions, there has been considerable confusion within the philosophical/ theological tradition about the proper or legitimate meaning of the term. One of the major tasks of contemporary theology is to try to clarify this confusion by analyzing the fundamental models or "root metaphors"[16] which underlie various theological and philosophical perspectives on the one hand, and different uses of the word "God" on the other, in order to get clear the implications of these various usages so decisions can be made as to which are consistent and legitimate and which are not.

Theology is basically "metaphysical" in character, in that it addresses itself to the formal analysis and clarification of an understanding of reality or the world, and the ultimate point of reference for that understanding. But theology is metaphysics with a special commitment and orientation, namely, to grasping that ultimate point of reference specifically as *God* and thus to setting out a picture of reality and the world which focuses in God. Theology does not begin with the general metaphysical task and proceed (eventually) to talk about God; it begins with the problem of the meaning of talk about God and then, in dealing with this problem, finds it must also address general metaphysical issues.

These observations put us into a position to understand the function of the rest of the technical theological vocabulary—words like "creation," "sin," "salvation," "faith," "trinity," "sacraments." Such terms provide the fundamental building blocks for constructing the overall theological conception of the world and humanity, a conception often articulated in the form of a "story."[17] They help to flesh out and give meaning to the concept of God by specifying how the ultimate point of reference is related to crucial dimensions of life; and God, in turn, can then be seen as the lynch-pin that holds together the whole world-view, informing every element and dimension as the source of being and meaning. We come back, thus, to a point made earlier. "God" is not an isolated term in the language, comprehensible in and by itself alone. Rather, it is the key term in a complex of meanings which is intended to grasp all experience and reality. It is this whole structure or complex of terms and meanings "presided over" by the term "God" that makes it possible to see all of life and the world as "under God." The special task of systematic theology is to spell out this world-view explicitly and in some detail.

V

What I have been arguing in this chapter can be summarized as follows:

(1) The roots of theology are not restricted to the life of the church or to special dogmas or documents venerated in the church, nor are they to be found in something as inchoate as "raw experience." They are to be found, rather, in the ordinary language(s) of Western culture at large, i.e., in the living speech of people for whom the word "God" has peculiar weight and significance.

(2) Theology as an activity and a discipline appears when critical attention is devoted to this word and the complex of meanings associated with it. The central business of theology is reflection on the peculiar weightiness and meaning involved in the term "God" with a view to determining as explicitly, precisely and coherently as possible just what that meaning is and what its implications are. Such reflection is logically prior to (though not empirically separable from) the addressing of any other theological issues or problems because the latter are to be understood as features or dimensions of the attempt to articulate a theological world-view as a whole; and the way in which they will be developed depends on how that whole is conceived or, at least, on how the ultimate point of reference for that whole, God, is conceived.

(3) Despite its logical priority, the concept of God cannot be developed independently of ancillary and secondary theological terms, for it gains its content by reference to them and its meaning through the particular explication and interpretation of life and the world which they articulate. It can be worked out, therefore, only in dialectical interrelationship and interdependence with what are taken to be other leading terms for articulating a theistic understanding of life and the world.

(4) Only with such careful attention to the complexity of the theological vocabulary does it become possible to do responsible theological work, whether that be the sketching out of a picture of the world and life as a whole in the form of a systematic theology, or the attention to particular doctrines, concepts or problems; whether it be conceived as explication of the experience or dogmas of the church or Bible, or as phenomenological description and interpretation of religious or general experience.

Unfortunately, much theological writing in past and present has been undertaken without first seriously considering these dialectical and logical complexities. In consequence the theological scene appears chaotic and confusing, expressing inconsistent and contradictory presuppositions and possessing no clear or obvious norms or criteria for sorting out or assessing them. What I have tried to do in this chapter is uncover and briefly sketch certain features of the logical structure which monotheistic theological conceptualization and reflection presuppose and within which they must work if they are to be intelligible and consistent. As we become more self-conscious about these presuppositions of our constructive theological work—whether we consider ourselves church theologians, philosophers of religion or reflective secular men and women—we may dare to hope that theology will gradually bring sufficient order into its house to enable it to perform, once again, truly significant services for the human community.

If my understanding of theology, as ultimately rooted in the common language and in general human experience, is correct, it has a general cultural significance; and there is no reason for it to be restricted to the parochial confines of the church or to be regarded as an esoteric or subrational discipline. Whether the church as an institution lives or dies, theology has an important cultural role to play—so long as people continue to use and understand the word "God."

It is possible, of course, that the word "God" will eventually die as a living and meaningful focus of attention and reflection. Would that be the end of theology as a mode of disciplined reflection? Two quite different alternative possible developments immediately come to mind. First, and most likely, the quest for formulation and understanding of an ultimate point of reference for grasping and interpreting human life and the world would go on, but it would employ different symbols than "God." What such symbols would be ("nature"? "being"? "life"?) or how they would function, we cannot now clearly conceive because no other symbol in Western languages has the depth and power and scope of "God"; so it is difficult to imagine just how another concept could substitute for it. Were such a development to take place, however, it is clear that what is presently done as "theology" would not disappear: the task of criticizing and reconstructing the "ultimate point of reference" would continue with the new primary symbol(s) as its focus.

One might raise the question, however, whether all interest in and attention to the problem of an ultimate point of reference might not disappear from human consciousness and culture, along with the active use of the word "God." Were this to happen, there would be an absolute demise of theology, not merely its transposition into some mode appropriate to newer symbolization. But what sort of human consciousness would this be that no longer asked after a way to understand human life as a whole, that no longer attempted to see the meaning of human experience in some unified way? Would consciousness utterly devoid of open-ended questioning, always pushing on beyond what is presently known and believed, be recognizably human?[18] Every culture of which we know has found it necessary to grasp and articulate the meaning of human existence in some mythical or metaphysical forms. Is a culture from which all such activity has completely dropped away, with life devoted wholly to the everyday, the hum-drum, the routine, really conceivable? Reflection on the ultimate point of reference for all life and thought and reality must surely go on in some form so long as human life persists. In the West such reflection has come to full self-consciousness pre-eminently in theological work; for this reason it falls especially to theology to see that critical and constructive investigation in this area be continued in a disciplined and fully responsible way.

---

[1]It is important that one not confuse the question of how one moves in theology from preliminary or penultimate issues to specifically theological ones—how one moves from talk about humanity or creation to talk about God—with the religious question of whether there is any "way from man to God" or only a way "from God to man" (Barth). Whatever may be the truth about the latter question regarding the grounds of salvation, it is clear that theology is a strictly human activity, a human mode of talk and reflection. Like other such human activities, it is subject to grammatical and logical and other humanly prescribed rules; it can be taught and learned, and the like. It is this question about the way we humans can and do talk about God, about what moves are required to undertake serious theological talk, that we are concerned with here, not the question about whether God is always accessible to us or whether he makes himself accessible only at his good-pleasure. The two issues are not fully separable, of course, because there is always the question whether certain speech about "God" is really about *God* or about some idol; and one might wish to contend that in cases of the latter sort it is not theology at all that is involved but rather some pseudo-theology. However, while this is certainly an important and legitimate issue it is one that can properly arise only farther down the road: before one can distinguish "genuine" theology from spurious, one must have some idea of what theology is; an imitation or a fake is parasitical on the real thing. Our investigation will have to begin, therefore, with the attempt to distinguish "theological" from other sorts of reflection and with the clarification of how one moves to undertake

specifically theological reflection. Only after that will we be in a position to attempt to distinguish between more and less adequate sorts of theology, between genuine and pseudo-theology.

[2]It should not be supposed that in thus characterizing theology I am referring only to traditional or Roman Catholic theologians. Such tradition-challenging Protestant theologians as Schleiermacher, Barth and Tillich all took the position that theology begins in and is essentially a work of and for the church. See F. Schleiermacher, *The Christian Faith* (Edinburgh: T. & T. Clark, 1928), §§2-19, and *Brief Outline of the Study of Theology* (Edinburgh: T. & T. Clark, 1850), Introduction and Part I; K. Barth, *Church Dogmatics*, I, 1(Edinburgh: T. & T. Clark, 1936), §§1-3; Paul Tillich, *Systematic Theology* I (Chicago: University of Chicago Press, 1951), pp. 1-18, 28-40.

[3]This is the typical modern approach to the problem of theology, and many of its basic lines were laid down by Schleiermacher. It appears to be gaining popularity again (after being somewhat in the shadow during the period of neo-orthodox dominance). Two recent (quite different) representatives of this approach are Langdon Gilkey, *Naming the Whirlwind* (Indianapolis: Bobbs-Merrill, 1969), and Richard R. Niebuhr, *Experiential Religion* (New York: Harper & Row, 1972).

[4]For a recent and very illuminating attempt to set out such a theory for theological purposes, see Edward Farley, *Ecclesial Man: A Social Phenomenology of Faith and Reality* (Philadelphia: Fortress Press, 1975), esp. chs. 4-5.

[5]No experience is completely pre-conceptual or pre-linguistic. On this point the pioneering work of Kant and Hegel, uncovering the heavy dependence of all experience on language and thought, has been largely confirmed by modern psychological and epistemological studies. This has again become an important theme in philosophy, particularly through the influence of Wittgenstein. For excellent recent summary discussions of these issues with reference to religious experience and language, see Paul Van Buren, *The Edges of Language* (New York: Macmillan, 1972), and John Bowker, *The Sense of God* (Oxford: Clarendon Press, 1973), ch. 7. The latter, which cites recent physio-neurological studies that show a certain priority of meaning and concept over "raw experience," is especially interesting in this connection.

[6]See W. C. Smith, *The Meaning and End of Religion* (New York: Mentor Books, 1964), pp. 162-64; and "Faith and Belief" (unpublished paper, 1968), pp. 14-18.

[7]It must be admitted, of course, that the theological reflection with which we are here concerned may be parochial to Western culture as a whole, for it is in the West that it grew up and in Western languages that its key words are found; and it cannot be taken for granted that strict parallels will be found everywhere else or even anywhere else. That is a problem which has not yet been sufficiently investigated: to see if other cultures have formed their experience and life in sufficiently analogous terms so that something like theology goes on there too, or can go on there; or whether it would be necessary to import what is largely Western vocabulary and conceptuality and imagery in order to do theology in a non-Western setting (as has been the case, for example, with much natural science). In this connection John Carman argues that in the Indian Vedanta tradition is to be found reflection very similar to Western theology. For discussion, see his recent book, *The Theology of Ramanuja* (New Haven: Yale University Press, 1974), esp. ch. 16. In any case, however, our present problem is not whether theology has universality in that broad sense. At this point I am simply contending that theology is and can be universal within Western culture, i.e., that all Westerners, simply by virtue of their cultural inheritance, have the necessary rudiments of vocabulary and conceptuality and imagery to begin engaging in theological investigation.

[8]For Ramsey's use of this phrase, see *Religious Language* (London: SCM Press, 1957), pp. 59-60.

[9]*Philosophical Investigations* (Oxford: Blackwell, 1958) I, §373.

[10]My own attempt to sketch out the structure of the Christian vocabulary will be found in *Systematic Theology: A Historicist Perspective* (New York: Scribner, 1968). I should observe, however, that at the time that book was written, I did not fully realize how radically Christian theology must be reconceived if it is understood as essentially imaginative construction. In consequence, although I am still prepared to defend the central material contention of that book—that the Christian faith and vocabulary are essentially "historicistic" in orientation—I now regard the methodological foundations of theology set forth there, especially as expressed in a somewhat simplistic view of "revelation," as seriously misleading.

[11]I want to emphasize that though I shall not be making use of sociological or linguistic surveys of the use of the term "God" in what follows, but base what I say on my sense of the language as a native English speaker, it would certainly be appropriate to test and verify my claims by the sort of careful studies that modern linguistics makes possible. The problem of the relation of the intuitive

grasp of proper linguistic use by a native speaker to the "objective" investigatory techniques available to modern linguistic science is a difficult one. For some discussion, see Benson Mates, "On the Verification of Statements about Ordinary Language," and Stanley Cavell, "Must We Mean What We Say?" in *Ordinary Language*, ed. V. C. Chappell (Englewood Cliffs, N.J.: Prentice-Hall, 1964); J. A. Fodor and J. J. Katz, "What is Wrong with the Philosophy of Language? " *Inquiry* (1962) 5:197-237, and "The Availability of What We Say," *Philosophical Review* (1963) 72:57-71; Zeno Vendler, *Linguistics in Philosophy* (New York: Cornell Univ. Press, 1967), ch. 1.

[12]It cannot be taken for granted that all "religious" talk or reflection is necessarily "theological," nor, for that matter, that all "theological" discussion will be "religious." For some discussion of certain of the distinctions to be kept in mind here, see my essays on "Secular, Religious and Theistic World-Views" and on "Christian Theology and the Scientific Study of Religion," in *God the Problem* (Cambridge: Harvard University Press, 1972).

[13]*Proslogium*, ch. 2.

[14]H. R. Niebuhr's phrase. See *Radical Monotheism and Western Culture* (New York: Harper and Row, 1960).

[15]I have argued this point particularly in *God the Problem*. Further discussion of the anthropomorphism of the idea of God will be found below in ch. 3.

[16]The term is Stephen Pepper's. See *World Hypotheses* (Berkeley: University of California Press, 1942), ch. 5.

[17]Certainly it was as a character in a story—taken at first to be Israel's story and later the story of all humankind—that God (Yahweh) first became a significant reality in human life and history; and it has been as a character in this story that God has continued to be believed in, worshipped and served by the large majority of his devotees. The basic framework of the Bible is narrative; and it is through God's "mighty deeds " recounted in this narrative that the impression of who God is, and what sort of character and expectations he has, has been deeply engraved on the Western consciousness. But God's reality (as suggested in the biblical story) was both too important and too complex for humans to be satisfied simply with the mythopoeic portrait in which he first became known. Critical questioning and systematic reconstruction of the biblical images and ideas, especially stimulated by the encounter with Greek philosophical traditions, soon produced the luxuriant growth of theological concepts and doctrines characteristic of the Christian era. And "God" thus became the keystone of systematic philosophical and theological conceptions of the world as well as the primary actor in the biblical drama. Because of this dual role, the theological vocabulary in terms of which God is expounded and interpreted is made up of concepts which draw upon both mythopoeic imagery and philosophical criticism and refinement. (For an illuminating analysis of the significance which the narrative mode of the biblical literature has had for the concept of God, together with a history of the problems which that mode has raised for modern theological reflection, see Hans Frei, *The Eclipse of Biblical Narrative* [New Haven: Yale University Press, 1974].)

[18]Cf. Karl Rahner, *Foundations of Christian Faith* (New York: Seabury Press, 1978), pp. 47–49.

2

Theology as Construction

"...it is your phantasy that creates the world for you, and...you can have no God without a world."

Friedrich Schleiermacher[1]

It may be supposed that theology should be conceived on analogy with modes of study such as psychology or biology: just as these latter seek to investigate the *logos* or structure of the soul or life, so theology seeks to clarify our talking and thinking about God. Each of these sciences has its own object, a reality existing over against and independently of the investigator, a reality to be perceived, studied, analyzed, theorized about, understood. The student of life has many examples—trees, dogs, birds, human beings—which can be examined; the student of the psyche has not only his or her own experience as object for reflection but also observations of the other persons round about. Likewise the theologian: though the object of inquiry here is not so directly evident and available, it too may be thought of as in some sense *there,* over against the theologian as an object of knowledge, as real as—actually, much more real than—any of the objects open to direct perception.

God, of course, is not directly perceivable: he cannot be "pointed out" as can ordinary objects of experience or easily evoked, like feelings or other inner states. Nevertheless, the concept of God has usually been treated as though it referred to a structure or reality that was definitely *there* and *given* (as objects of experience are there and given); God exists independently of the perceiver or knower and has a definite character which can be in some measure described. In short, God is (despite all careful qualifications and disclaimers) conceived on the model of a perceivable object; more specifically, on the model of a person who can speak and act. (This is not difficult to understand when one remembers that theological reflection had its origins in myths in which God and the gods were pictured as perceivable beings that walked and talked with men and women, spoke in human tongues, performed various particular actions.) Of course no sophisticated theologian has regarded God as simply a very large and powerful person, living in and ruling from some heaven above; nevertheless, the model which has determined the logical character of the concept of God was that of an object over against us (substance with attributes, subject to which predicates could be assigned), the sort of reality that ordinarily comes to be known in some relatively direct quasi-experiential way.[2]

The concept of the world, God's creation, usually has had a similar logical standing. Though much more complex and full than any ordinary object of perception, it was still essentially a kind of *thing* that was what it was, a very large and complicated object, containing within itself all the other objects of experience, and men and women as well. No one has ever been in a position directly to perceive the world as such; but this is simply because we are within it: if it were possible to get outside the world and have a look at it—as on a space ship one can see the earth floating in the distance—then the world too would become an object for direct perception. (The fact that "world" can denote *earth*—a definitely perceivable object as well as universe, doubtless contributes to this sense of its being the name of some kind of definite object.) Though no thoughtful writer believed that the world was literally simply a very large thing, the grammatical and logical forms in which the concept was handled were those derived from and created for our speaking about and reflection upon objects of perception. Thus, the model on the basis of which the concepts of both God and world were constructed and employed was that of the perceivable, independently existing person or object.

It is not difficult to understand the task of theology on this presupposition. It is to make as clear as possible (as a biologist might seek to make clear what a tree is, or an astronomer what the sun is) just what kind of realities God and the world are, showing, of course, how they are interrelated and interconnected with each other. Doctrines of

God's aseity and creative activity, his work sustaining the world in being and his providential guidance of history, were all developed to this end; conversely, conceptions of the world's creatureliness and contingency, of human sin and the need for redemption, explored these same relations from the other side. Despite all claims that we human beings can never come to know God in his essence, what was in fact presented by theologians was an elaborate scheme of interpretation which set out what it was believed God actually was, and what humanity and the world were, and how they were related to each other.

An important feature of this scheme was the belief that God was a quasi-personal being, and in particular that he possessed knowledge (or truth) perfect knowledge of all things in all respects. This was in sharp contrast with men and women who frequently fell into error and whose sin, many thought, imprisoned them in falsehood and untruth. It was not really possible, therefore, for humans on their own to come to an adequate understanding of themselves, the world, or of God. Such understanding was the possession of God alone and could be had by them only if God chose to communicate it. Since God was thought of anthropomorphically as a "speaking being," such divine revelation was possible and had, it was believed, in fact occurred. Hence, whatever true knowledge men and women have—at least with regard to the ultimate questions about God, themselves and the world—will be what they have received from God. In any case, the standard for all questions of truth is the objective reality of God's own knowledge, not anything directly within the grasp of finite human beings. Truth, therefore, was also conceived as having a kind of objectivity, or overagainstness; it was a quality or attribute or possession of (the objectively existing) God. The human mind had to conform itself to this objective reality of God's truth if it was to avoid falling into error.

This whole scheme was consistent in itself; and it was the basis for a coherent conception of the theological task, one that has in fact been operative through most Western history. The theologian's task consisted, on the one hand, of setting out clearly and fully this schema itself, so it would be possible to see just how God, humankind and the world are interrelated and interconnected. On the other hand, the theologian was concerned to show how and why this schema is *true*, i.e., is an accurate reflection of God's Truth, either as God has himself revealed that truth to men and women (e.g., in the Bible) or as we have come to know that truth in some other way (through intuition or experience). There were, of course, great disagreements about details of all these matters, and splits between Augustinians and Pelagians, Catholics and Protestants, high churchmen, low churchmen, mystics and biblicists, and others, proliferated. But nearly all accepted the basic schema which elaborated a conception of God, and of God's Truth, as having independence and objectivity over against humanity.

I

I have suggested that the presupposition of this approach to theology has been the acceptance of a model for conceiving God and God's Truth which is based on the objectivity and overagainstness of the object of perception. Sophisticated writers, of course, have not held that God could be directly "seen" like yonder tree; nonetheless, his objectivity was often conceived on that model. This raised—and raises—some difficult problems. With a perceivable object, we put together our concept on the basis of abstraction and generalization from percepts; but if there are no direct percepts of God how—and out of what—is this concept constructed? As long as the basic schema is unquestioned, this problem remains concealed by belief in revelation; God has *revealed* himself and the truth about (concept of) himself to humankind, so our knowledge of God has a firmer foundation, if anything, than ordinary experiential knowledge. It does not depend upon the vagaries and errors of ordinary perception and cognition but comes right from God himself. However, when the validity or truth of the claims about revelation begin to be doubted, the entire schema starts to break down. It becomes necessary to develop other ways of understanding how the concept of God is constructed in human consciousness.

Several alternatives have presented themselves. Some have held that the concept of God is a part of the basic equipment of the human mind, an "innate idea" which the mind always has available to itself and with which it naturally works in developing its conceptions of the world and the human. Others have contended that the idea of God is developed as a kind of explanatory hypothesis to account for the existence and character of the world (or of some feature[s] of the world) as we grasp it in our experience. Some, working out the implications of the model drawn from ordinary perception, have been prepared to argue that it is developed on the basis of a peculiar or special "religious experience" in which God is somehow directly encountered or known.

There are problems peculiar to each of these positions which I cannot go into here; a major difficulty common to them all, however, and characteristic also of the more traditional position, was the failure to recognize certain peculiarities of the logical status and function of the concept of God. It was Kant who first pointed out the root difficulties, but his revolutionary insights remain unappropriated in much theological work.

Kant saw that ideas like "God" and "world" performed a different kind of function in our thinking than concepts like "tree" or "man." While the latter are used to organize and classify elements of experience directly, thus helping to make possible experience itself and serving as the vehicles through which experience is cognized, the former "regulative ideas" function at a remove from direct perception or experience: they are used for ordering and organizing our conceptions or knowledge. The "world," for example, is never an object of direct perception; it is, rather, a concept with which we hold together in a unified totality all our experience and knowledge of objects— everything having its own proper place "within" the world. Kant showed that insoluble antinomies arise when the world is treated as itself an object, like the objects of experience: Did the world have a beginning in time? or has it existed for all eternity? Is it infinite in extent, or finite? Is it infinitely divisible, or made up of ultimate indivisible elements? These questions, which are simply unanswerable when the world is treated as an objective reality, are dissolved when we recognize that the concept of world is a construct of the mind, a heuristic device by means of which the mind orders its own contents but the objective referent for which we have no way of discovering.

For Kant the concept of God, also a construct, has even wider application than the concept of world. It functions, on the one hand, as the ultimate unifier of all experience and concepts both subjective and objective ("world" unifies only the concepts of "objects"), and, on the other, as the most fundamental postulate of the moral life, that which makes moral experience intelligible by rendering the world in which we act a moral universe. Even less than "world," then, could "God" be an object of experience, or a reality conceivable on the model of a perceivable object. It is the mind's most profound and highest creation, that by means of which it brings unity and significance into all dimensions of its life. To regard God as some kind of describable or knowable object over against us (as in the schema on which most theology has been based) is at once a degradation of God and a serious category error.

We need not explore here the elaborate argument with which Kant buttressed his analysis, nor examine the insights or the problems that arose from his attempt to work out the details. For our purposes, the importance of Kant was his discovery that the concepts or images of God and the world are imaginative constructs, created by the mind for certain intra-mental functions and, thus, of a different logical order than the concepts and images which we have of the objects of experience. The developments since Kant in epistemology and the psychology of knowing have confirmed his work here. We now know that all our perception is heavily colored by the interpretive schemes carried in language and culture, that we never perceive objects immediately, uninterpreted by a conceptual framework created by the human imagination. Concepts like "God" and "world," which hold together the whole fabric of a culture's understanding of life and reality, are created only over many generations as men and women seek to make sense of their experience in the terms bequeathed by their ancestors. These notions are thus continually and gradually reshaped and remade into broader, more flexible, and more powerful instruments for bringing order into life and experience.

It should occasion no surprise that there is no percept that corresponds directly to our concept of God. That concept was in the making from the time of Abraham and before, and it binds together and unifies the overall experience and life of all those intervening generations. It intends to point to that which is in and under and behind all things everywhere and always, "the Creator of all things visible and invisible." Little wonder, then, that it does not correspond to anything we can directly perceive or know and that it must be constructed in the mind and through history by processes quite different from those which produce an ordinary concept.[3]

The treatment of the concept of God as though it referred to some sort of object or entity was characteristic of much traditional theology. It was assumed that God or the divine exists or has reality "out there," i.e., as distinct from and independent of human beings and human thinking about God; it was taken for granted that the name "God" refers to a "real being."[4] The problem of salvation was how the divine—the only truly Real reality—could be appropriated by the human, how our mortality could put on immortality. And so various schemes of salvation—through the sacraments, through belief in Christ's victory over the devil, through attitudes of faith and trust in God—were developed. It is God, the divine, the Other over against us, who in his grace is the source or giver of salvation; we are simply its humble recipients. This whole mode of thought takes the objectivity of God for granted.[5]

However, such a sharp distinction of God and humanity also raises questions about whether we have in fact appropriated the divine gift of salvation, how it can be united with a sinful nature like ours. It would seem that our nature must become changed into the divine, else it would be forever lost in its present state of sin. And yet how can it become in some way divinized and still remain *our* nature? Luther faced these problems in their most profound and existential form, and his position represents the ultimate *reductio ad absurdum* of objectivist hypostasizing theological language.[6] A change does not occur in us at all in salvation; we are not *made* righteous by God's grace. Rather, righteousness remains with God and with Christ and is simply "imputed" to us. Everything belongs to God, nothing to us, in this transaction. This can then become the ground for Luther's confidence: he no longer needs to worry whether he has become a different man or whether he has become righteous: whether he has or not is not to the point. The only thing that matters is the objective righteousness and faithfulness of God over against him; this is imputed to him and he can depend on it unconditionally. Men and women are thus freed from any reliance on themselves or on their own works; and they can go about their tasks in this world without worrying whether they will perform them in such a way as to enhance their salvation, their relation to the divine Other over against them.

Luther's position depends on the most radical distinction between God and humanity, God and the world, each being entities or realities in no way to be confused with the other, entities which cannot in any way be mixed or combined with the other. (The notion of an entity as that with very sharp or distinct boundaries setting it off from everything else seems clearly presupposed.) This position is a *reductio ad absurdum*, I suggest, because it makes the distinction so sharp that even my consciousness of God—my ideas about him or the quality of my faith in him has nothing whatever to do with the question of my salvation.[7] God has indeed become "wholly other" here. Confidence in such a God can undoubtedly overcome all the insecurity of the finite and relative, for

God is wholly other than all of that; and for this reason Luther's position still has great religious power for many. But the sharp distinction which Luther makes implies that nothing in us—even our thoughts about God—can claim actually to relate us to him, i.e., can lay claim to being valid or true or dependable in any respects. In short, God becomes—if one works through consistently what is entailed here—an absolutely unknowable, incomprehensible, unattainable, mysterious "X." While this frees us to live out our lives in this world with confidence and spontaneity, it also means that nothing we are or can be, nothing we do or can do, nothing we think or can think, can in any way affect our relation to God either positively or negatively. God has become so abstracted from our consciousness and experience that these can go on, indeed, must go on, without reference to him or thought about him: he has become a zero, a nothing, a complete irrelevancy to our life here and now.

Obviously Luther did not draw these conclusions, nor do others who still find his position existentially meaningful, but the steady movement toward secularism in the West since the Reformation did. It became clear—and this is Luther's great importance—that to take with absolute seriousness the completely objective reference of our concept of God, so that our subjective ideas, attitudes and activities have nothing whatever to do with what or who God is, empties the notion of God of all specifiable meaning. Luther himself did not notice this (though he did emphasize God's "hiddenness") because he took over much of the traditional content of the idea of God uncritically, supposing it not to consist of mere human opinions and constructs but to describe what God had revealed himself really to be "out there" in his own being. But in the centuries which followed, this point could no longer be overlooked. It became clear that there was no way to jump out of our idea of God—our construct of God—to God himself as an objective reality. If God is really completely objective to and distinct from all our ideas, he is irrelevant to us in every respect; and we may as well lead our lives with no reference to or concern about him. This is the secularistic conclusion which can be drawn from Luther's position.

However, Luther's *reductio ad absurdum* of the objectivist language also opened up—all unbeknownst to him, and to the consternation of latter-day objectivists like Karl Barth—another alternative, namely, the understanding that "God" is not a reality over against us, totally other from us at all, but is in fact a construct of the human imagination which performs certain important functions in our thinking and experience. The only God we can know or respond to or take account of is the God *we* can know and take account of and respond to. It is the God that we, with the help of a long tradition developing before us, construct in our imagination as the ultimate point of reference for all life and thought and reality. Luther represents the spectacular climax and, at the same time, the beginning of an irreversible breakdown, of talk about God in objectifying terms. With Kant the issue at last became clarified: "God" must be understood as a human construct, doubtless a very important, perhaps indispensable, construct, but a human construct nonetheless.

Successors to Kant—Feuerbach, Nietzsche, Freud, Dewey—have seized upon his discovery that "God" is an imaginative construct and have argued what some have regarded as an atheistic case. I do not wish to debate here the validity of such interpretations, but will grant that it is possible to put Kant's discovery to an atheistic use. But it is not necessary to take this position, and the possibility of it should not blind us to the correctness of Kant's fundamental claim. Though it is true that God's reality can no longer be thought of on the model of the objectivity of perceivable things, the question remains open whether the concept of God does not refer to reality in some other— more profound sense. Kant himself, as is well known, drew this conclusion, holding that God's reality was necessarily presupposed by the self in its stance as actor and moral agent. We cannot, however, explore Kant's reflections on this matter here, for we must attempt to discern what this new understanding of the peculiar character of the concepts of God and world means for the task of theology.

II

As long as theologians suppose they are engaged in a kind of "science" which is concerned basically with attempting to describe its "object" in straightforward terms, much as physicists and biologists describe theirs, the issues will tend to be formulated so as to focus attention on just what the object of theology might be. Here everyone and anyone can come forth with his or her own claims, and there is no court in which they can be adjudicated: we simply do not have access to a theological "object" in this sense at all, making it possible to distinguish the invalid and unreliable from the significant and true. This way lies both obscurantism and chaos—precisely the situation we find in the contemporary scene.

If this condition is to be overcome, it is essential for us to recognize that the peculiar logical status of the central concepts with which theology deals demands radical reconception of both the task of theology and the way in which that task is carried out. Theology can no longer conceive of itself as presenting straightforwardly a kind of picture or map of *how things are*—the old schema of God, humankind and the world in their structural relations with each other. Rather, theology must conceive its work as more like building a house: using materials given in experience it is in fact *constructing a world* the fundamental design of which is not found in the materials themselves but is employed to give them a significant order and meaning. "World" and "God" are not objects directly describable but are constructs or images by means of which men and women: (a) conceive or picture the multiplicity and plurality of experience and life as having some unity, order and wholeness (the concept or image of world) and (b) grasp this ordered context of life not as ultimately threatening or even as merely neutral with respect to what is humanly valuable and meaningful, but as informed by purpose, meaning and loving care (the concept or image of God).

To regard God and the world as constructs with which we bring order and personal meaning into experience does not involve downgrading them in comparison with directly-perceivable objects. On the contrary. As defining the context within which the objects of experience are given us, they provide both the basis for our fundamental orientation in life and the chief source of those principles of interpretation by means of which we discern what is of significance or meaning among all the stimuli impinging upon us. They thus have great *practical* import for us; indeed, we could not live and act and think at all without some such ordering principles or images; and we would certainly have no way to deal with crisis or catastrophe. The constructive work of the mind through which humans have produced world-pictures and mythologies is no optional or dispensable speculative activity: it brings about the ordering of experience in such a way as to make it possible to see meaning in it, to see what place human life has within the whole of reality, and thus to see what we can do, how we should act. Without the development of overarching concepts and comprehensive images and stories, we would have no basis for selecting, from among all the potential objects of attention impinging upon us, those which can be ordered and combined into a pattern of sufficient structure and meaning to make possible conscious, coherent, human life. The concepts or images of God and world perform ordering and meaning-bestowing functions of this sort in Western culture. In the position I am sketching here they remain, thus, absolutely central—that toward which, and in terms of which, all life and thinking is to be oriented—but now they are understood not as realities that are simply *there*, like ordinary perceivable objects, but rather as essential constructs without which we could not live or act.

An analogy may be useful. Charts and models are always our constructions of a reality which is too immense, or otherwise inaccessible, to grasp without their aid. They consist of imaginative systematic orderings of selected items and elements, so brought into relation and interconnection with each other as to emphasize and thus make clearly visible to us certain features which we might otherwise overlook or not recognize at all. In some cases we can discern how closely or accurately they set forth the real structure of that which they represent; for example, with an architect's blueprints for a house the relations of chart to object are precisely definable and measurable. But in other cases this is not possible at all: the relation of the models of waves and particles to those features of the actual structure of matter (or energy?) which we designate as "electrons" is impossible to specify; and the concept of electron is itself a very complex construct of the mind. We build up or develop these maps or models in accordance with our interest or need to move or act in certain ways. The model or concept is constructed so as to eliminate material irrelevant to these particular concerns, highlighting that which we take to be especially pertinent. Whether this accurately represents the "actual structure" of the "object-in-itself" (i.e., the object conceived as abstracted completely from all our needs, concerns and interests) no one can say; and it really does not matter at all. The map is a good one if it enables us to get where we are trying to go: a geological map of oil deposits in North Dakota would be useless to a tourist simply trying to drive through the state, just as a road map would be of no help to the oil well driller. Of course it is clear that a useful map or model cannot be simply a fabrication of its maker's imagination; it must select and display certain elements or features of the "reality" it represents in such a way as to enable its user actually to progress toward his or her goal. But beyond that, the degree to which it presents the "actual structure" of what is "really there" often cannot be determined.

It is similar with the constructs "world" and "God." However important they may be for thinking about life and ordering existence and action, we can have no way of knowing to just what they refer or how accurately they represent it. We never encounter the world as an object of perception which can be examined, measured, experimented with. All our examining and experimenting takes place *within* the world, where we ourselves are also located as constituent elements, and just what this whole is within which all else is found we can only speculate or guess. Of course our speculation is not entirely free and uncontrolled here: the world must be conceived as the kind of "place" within which all these events can indeed happen, but this leaves its boundaries and structure very vague. Nevertheless, "world" is a concept (or category) without which we could not do, for it gives experience that fundamental order and unity apart from which it would not be coherent enough to be experience at all. This is why every culture known to modern investigators, no matter how primitive, possesses myths which set out pictures of the world within which the life of that people is lived, and which provide fundamental guidance and orientation for that life.

The concept of God (in the Judaeo-Christian sense) is not indispensable to human life in the way that of world is. It developed in the historical streams that produced Western civilization, but it has come to play an important role in other cultures as well. Where it has been significant it has complicated and qualified the meaning of the concept of world, with which it stands in tandem.[8] "God created the world" means that the world gains its being and its fundamental forms of order from a source outside of, or beyond, itself, that the deepest roots of the order within which life must be lived are not immanent in the world itself but have been (and are being) imposed upon it or gifted to it from without. The principal model which has informed the concept of this relation—creative activity (in contrast with, for example, generation or eruption or interaction of cosmic forces) is based upon the human experience of bringing into being new forms of reality through work, through cultivation and the construction of artifacts. This model, if taken at all literally, easily suggests the objectifying schema which lies at the base of most Western theology. (Cf. Genesis 2 where the myth has God modelling Adam out of clay and planting the earth like a garden; also Genesis 1 where God speaks powerful words that bring into being whole orders of reality objective to him.) Consequently, it is no surprise to discover that God easily becomes conceived in anthropomorphic and objectifying terms, as a knowing, willing, purposive being who stands outside of or beyond the world, a world which he has created and within which he continues to act to realize longstanding objectives of his own.

In this schema the world and all its contents (all of "creation") can be properly understood only in relation to the external divine purposes and activity that brought them into being. And, therefore, adequate orientation in life for human beings cannot be found with reference to the world taken simply by itself: it derives from awareness of and conformity to God's will and action. Moreover, in this scheme the world is a dynamic growing reality, still undergoing change and development at God's hands as he works toward the realization of his ultimate objectives; and men and women must grasp the meanings of their own lives and their proper tasks in life within the context of this developing historical order. History is moving forward toward goals yet unrealized, goals perhaps unclear to those living within it, and life's meaning will be found only through constructive and significant participation in this forward-thrusting movement. Inasmuch as this whole movement is regarded as fundamentally a humanizing or personalizing of the world and of humanity—God is working toward his perfect "kingdom," a community ordered by love in which men and women find genuine fulfillment—cooperation with and service of God is conceived as serving humankind's own ultimate best interests.

Let us now prescind from the quasi-mythical form in which the relations of God and world are here expressed and observe what has happened to the concept of the world with the introduction of the concept of God. The concept of God functions here in such a way as to qualify or transform the bare meaning of world, so that the latter is grasped as of the profoundest human significance. In any view, of course, the world has human significance; it is the place where men and women live. But in a theistic view its significance for humanity is much deeper than that: the world is no hostile or threatening prison from which men and women must somehow escape in order to find fulfillment in life (e.g., Platonism, gnosticism), nor is it a merely neutral environment which has more or less accidentally brought forth humankind along with many other species of life (modern evolutionary doctrine) and which will ultimately swallow them up once again. The world is, rather, the intended consequence of God's continuing purposive and humane work; that is, it is seen as the appropriate "home" for human beings, a context for human life pervaded and ordered by a "purposiveness" and "love" which will make possible genuine human fulfillment. In this view, thus, the world is invested with the deepest possible humane meaning and value, and human life—with its character as conscious and intentional, and with its longing for genuine understanding, love, and communion—is seen to be grounded ultimately in a hospitable cosmic order, an order symbolized in terms of the purposes, love and care of a fundamentally personal God.

III

As long as the concept of God was taken to represent a kind of "object" that simply was what it was, the world being another similar "object" which God had "created" and on which he was continuing to "act," the task of the theologian was fundamentally descriptive and expository: he or she was to set out the theological schema as clearly as possible in whatever detail was allowed by the revelation vouchsafed to the church, drawing such conclusions as would illuminate the proper ordering of human life. Even when understood in this way, however, theology was primarily an activity of construction—construction of a conception or picture of God, of human life and of the world. The criteria guiding that construction were drawn from a variety of sources: from the biblical picture of God, with exegetical considerations assuming considerable prominence; from the belief that God is righteous, merciful and forgiving, with moral experience and reflection contributing significantly; from the concern to find a secure foundation for human life, or an explanation of the universe, or an appropriate object of worship. These and other considerations all influenced (often unconsciously) construction of the idea of God. Since the radically constructive character of theological work went unrecognized, however, theologians were unable to focus clearly on the human purposes or functions it served; nor could they conceive or address the question of what criteria would be most appropriate for guiding and evaluating this constructive activity.

As we have seen, the ideas of God and the world are constructed by the human imagination for essentially practical purposes: in order to live and act it is necessary to have some conception or picture of the overall context, the fundamental order, within which human life falls.

The ideas and images of God and the world have supplied this in the West; in other cultures other images and conceptions—some rather similar, others very different—have done this work. All such notions or pictures are created primarily to provide orientation in life; to suppose that they represent in any straightforward or one-to-one way "how things are" is a serious mistake.

Once these facts are recognized, theology must work along different lines than in the past. It will no longer be engaged in searching out the channels of our "knowledge of God" (on analogy with other "knowledge"), then setting out a description of what is given through those channels; theological construction is of a different sort, and requires quite different criteria, from the construction of concepts of ordinary objects, where we are concerned whether our concepts do justice to what is actually perceived under certain appropriate conditions. The purpose of theological construction is to produce concepts (and world-pictures and stories) which make possible adequate orientation in life and the world. Of proposed concepts of God and world, therefore, one must ask such questions as these: What forms of human life do these conceptions of its context facilitate? which forms inhibit? What possibilities do they open up for men and women? which do they close off? Like a map guiding the traveler through unfamiliar territories—or better: like a compass which faithfully points a direction of orientation in the uncharted regions where the traveler through life must move—the concepts of God and world must be assessed and reconstructed in consideration of the kinds of activity and forms of experience they make possible, rather than with reference to some objects to which they are supposed to "correspond."

The theologian's task is to construct a conception or picture of the world—the whole that contains all that is and all that can be conceived—as pervaded by and purveying a particular kind of (humane) meaning and significance because of its grounding in an ultimately humane reality. In this respect the theologian is essentially an artist; and the activity of imaginative unifying and ordering in which he or she is engaged is to some extent controlled by aesthetic considerations of harmony and balance, consistency and contrast. However, unlike much art, theology does not confine itself to this or that segment or fragment of experience, attempting to set it forth clearly and distinctly, but rather addresses itself to the *whole* within which all experience falls. In painting his or her picture of the whole, the theological artist must draw on wide ranges and types of experience, showing how each is grasped in the integrating vision and what each means, for the "whole" is nothing, an empty abstraction, apart from the parts that make it up. Moreover, the picture which results dare not be highly idiosyncratic or "subjective"; it must be recognizably of our world, our life, our experience. It will have to find place for the terrors and joys, the triumphs and failures, the striving and the repose, the loves and hatreds of actual human life. It will have to do justice to the complexity of political and economic institutional structures in an industrial society, as well as to the intimacy of personal communion; it will have to deal with and be relevant to problems of conservation of the environment on this planet as well as personal crises of despair and meaninglessness. No important dimension of experience can be omitted from the theologian's concern and interest and interpretation, and he or she must exert every effort to root out one-sidedness, prejudice and bias. In these respects theological work attempts to be descriptive and scientific and "objective," and it is dependent on the natural and social sciences, and history, for knowledge of the facts.

It should not be supposed that the theologian creates the order into which he or she fits the multifarious features and dimensions of life simply *ex nihilo*. Such an arbitrarily constructed world would have little plausibility or significance and could hardly provide a context for ongoing human life or for active religious worship or devotion. The theologian's task of constructing a meaningful and humane world is in part the task of articulating and explicitating a world already in certain respects defined in and by the culture in its religious traditions, its (conscious and unconscious) myths, its rituals and taboos, its linguistic classifications;[9] that is, it is always based on the prior human constructive activity which produced and shaped the culture. Insofar as the theologian is drawing upon what is already explicit in tradition and what is implicit in accepted myth and ritual, he or she is engaged more in discovering something given in the culture than in creating something new. But to the extent that the theologian's articulation involves making sharp and clear what had previously not been consciously recognized and expressed and defined, thus drawing lines and boundaries for consciousness and reflection and action which had not existed before, his or her activity clearly involves the creation or construction of new concepts of God, and of the world as "under God."

The finished product of the theologian's constructive work is not, like many works of art, essentially something external to the artist, an optional object available in the public arena to be viewed or heard. Rather this work of art is to be *lived in:* it is the very form and meaning of human life which is here being constructed and reconstructed. Theological work must thus have a universality and comprehensiveness which does not necessarily obtain for the artist, and it must find a kind of public acceptance as a proper home in which to live. Metaphysical (and/ or mythological) ideas are absolutely indispensable to humans for orientation in life. We have a right, then, indeed a necessity, to construct them in such a way as to portray the world as sufficiently meaningful for us to live and act.

To say theology is largely constructive activity does not mean that it is empty or untrue or dealing with the unreal. When it is the "whole" with which we are concerned, the only "reality" or "truth" available to us will be the product of the mind's powers of imaginative synthesis or construction; the adequacy and truth of high-level, all-inclusive notions like "world" or "God"—or, for that matter, "nature" or "being"—can never be ascertained by recourse to the "things themselves" to see how well and in what respects our ideas "correspond." Here we are dealing with concepts that in some way refer to, or comprehend, every item and possibility of both experience and imagination: everything that exists is included within the world, and God is "the Creator of all things visible and invisible." We simply do not have, and cannot even conceive what it would be like to have, any direct experience or perception of realities of this order of universality and comprehensiveness. Hence, theological issues must be adjudicated in ways other than those appropriate to the concepts of, and statements about, the objects of experience.

Some may object to this formulation of the theological task on the ground that it seems to make the theologian's work subjective and arbitrary, rather than coming to terms with the claim that it is ultimate reality or God—that which determines itself and which is not subject to human making or remaking—which is the proper theological subject-matter. However, such an objection has force only on an erroneous presupposition. It fails to note that the idea of "that which determines itself and which is not subject to human making or re-making" is itself a complex construct. Reality of this order of abstraction does not become known to us directly in perception or intuition but only conceptually through the mind's creation of a complex concept which includes such abstract elements as self-determination, independence from the human, and contrast with everything contingent and conditioned. How else than imaginatively or in idea could the utterly universal and the radically other and independent be represented to us? Imaginative construction is the proper mode—indeed, the only mode—through which we can become aware of God in his full autonomy and self-integrity. Once we recognize that all notions like "ultimate reality" or "God" or "being itself" are human creations made possible by exercise of the mind's highest powers of imagination, idealization and conceptualization, we will understand that the issue is not between accepting the given as it "really is" or making our own world, but rather the question of what sort of world we will construct. The answer to that surely must be: a world within which we can live—fruitfully, meaningfully, creatively, freely. "I came that they may have life, and have it abundantly" (John 10:10).

IV

Since the radically constructive character of the theological task has not been clearly recognized in the past, there is little in the tradition to give us guidance on how to proceed methodologically. This is not because earlier theologians (including among these for the moment biblical writers, prophets and apostles, as well as teachers in the church and synagogue) were not themselves engaged in similar constructive activity—surely the work of an Amos or a Paul, of an Augustine or a Luther must be regarded as contributing to the construction and reconstruction of the notion of God—but rather because they did not understand themselves as creative in this way. On the contrary, they took themselves to be but vessels of the Holy Spirit, receptive to the activity of the Creator and Redeemer God, but not themselves the productive sources of their work; indeed, they would have repudiated this latter idea as—if true—the grossest sort of hubris or a clear case of idolatry. Accordingly, there was not occasion for them to reflect on the methods or criteria of theological construction, though they themselves were actively engaged in it.

Are these charges of hubris and idolatry not proper ones to be brought against this essay? Does not the conception of theology as construction turn God into our creation, our contrivance, our tool, to be made as we like and used as we like? How are the claims that God is absolutely independent, the source and ground of all else, the only proper center of life, one who can be known only through his own initiative in self-revelation, to be reconciled with the attempt to develop criteria and procedures that will enable us to gain more definite control over our theological activity?

This way of putting the matter is rooted in a confusion about the stance of religious devotion. Since in worship a devotee may bow in awe before God, acknowledging all life and meaning as his gracious gift, it may be supposed that the posture of the lowly creature abasing himself or herself before the Creator is the only one proper to devotion. But theology, also, has its origins in devotion to God. A deep respect for, and concern about, who God really is may give rise to a profound awareness of the inadequacy of the symbolical forms with which the religious tradition has articulated and communicated its faith. This may lead to sharp criticism of those forms and thence to the construction of new concepts and images. All this will naturally be disturbing to the unreflective believer, for it is not easy for religious faith to become more self-conscious and self-critical about that to which it devotes itself. But only through doing so can it overcome its often naive, inhuman and idolatrous conceptions of God, thus gradually developing images and concepts genuinely worthy of human worship. The object to which the unreflective mind has given itself in devotion has changed over the centuries as the insights of critical reflection were gradually incorporated into the concepts and images on which faith fed—as, that is, the imaginative construct to which devotion gave itself changed.

Even granting this importance of theological criticism and construction, however, questions about hubris and idolatry might still be raised in face of the bald claim that the concept of God is entirely our construct. Such a claim seems to suggest that it is merely our arbitrary contrivance, invented by us for our purposes and to be used by us in any way that seems convenient.

The problem here arises from supposing that theological conceptual construction is a completely free and arbitrary activity, that we can make our words and ideas do whatever we please. But that is obviously false. Words and concepts have meanings and uses in the language we have inherited which we ignore at our peril. They each have an integrity of their own, which we cannot violate without destroying the possibility of communication and even of our own clear thinking. Though they are all human "constructs," they may not be used arbitrarily but only in accordance with certain rules (grammatical, syntactical, logical, semantic), if they are to do their proper work for us. The rules also, of course, are human creations, but they admit even less of arbitrary disregard in fruitful and significant work. The concept of God, above all others, indicating as it does reality with radical independence and aseity, the ultimate point of reference for all life and thinking, is simply not at our disposal to construct any way we please. Serious theology will seek to uncover the constituents that give this notion its special meaning and the criteria which govern its use. If and as that is done, it may be possible to construct—or better, to reconstruct— that concept with greater precision and adequacy.

Theology has always been a constructive activity; it has always been concerned with formulating and reformulating the concept of God and its implications for all human life, in the most adequate and appropriate way possible. Once this is recognized, it becomes clear that the central problem of theological method is to discern and formulate explicit criteria and procedures for theological construction.

The demand for *criteria* here results from a recognition that the constructions of God which we have received out of the past—constructions of poet, mythmaker, prophet, theologian and philosopher—have all too often been arbitrary and idiosyncratic, influenced by fundamentally irrelevant or disastrously misleading psychological and cultural conditions, as well as by racial, sexual, ethnocentric and self-centered biases and prejudices of all sorts. Our theological "treasure [is] in earthen vessels" (2 Cor 4:7) which are far from adequate to contain and express what they intend. Hence, continuous reassessment of their adequacy, their validity and their appropriateness must be undertaken. Thus the attempt to engage in self-conscious theological construction, and to clarify and state explicitly the criteria on the basis of which such construction should proceed, is an effort to attain greater objectivity in theology—i.e., greater faithfulness to theology's proper subject-matter—not a retreat into subjectivity or arbitrariness or fancy. It requires us to get as clear as we possibly can just what it is we are trying to say when we say "God " and to reduce as far as possible the influence of unconscious confusions and prejudicial biases in our talk and thinking.

V

To what point has our argument brought us? I can conveniently draw together the various threads of this chapter by distinguishing several levels on which theological work may be thought to proceed. *First-order theology* (which I have been arguing is no longer appropriate, or perhaps even possible) is carried out when it is supposed that the theologian's task is to set forth as adequately as possible a picture of God, humankind and the world *as they are*, as though they were objects over against us which in some way could be described .

First-order theology originated in the myth-making activities of primal men and women who attempted to find orientation for life by developing imaginative stories and world-pictures. These cosmic legends and maps were modified and elaborated over many generations, and they provided frameworks of interpretation within which life could be carried on and understood. It was not clearly recognized, of course, in primal societies, that the myths and maps produced were constructs of the human imagination: such an understanding could appear only much later in human history, with the development of a clearer consciousness of the distinction between subject and object. Hence, the gods were taken to be real and active, the most important realities with which human beings had to do.

First-order theology, however, is not confined to primal cultures which fail to make a clear distinction between subject and object. It becomes even more pronounced when theologians (or believers)—with that distinction in mind—take theological constructs to be more or less adequate representations of objective realities. Most theology done in the West until the time of Kant, Schleiermacher and Hegel (despite misgivings about objectivism particularly in Platonistic traditions)[10] must be regarded as first-order; even since the work of these men much theology has continued in that mode.

When awareness arises that theological concepts are fundamentally imaginative constructs rather than abstractions or generalizations or deductions from percepts, we move to *second-order theology*. Now the crucial questions appear to be not simply, Do our concepts correspond to the objects they claim to represent? but rather: What is the ground or justification for making this kind of construction? What alternative constructs are available, and how might they be justified? This is the period of comparative religion and comparative theologies, when it is recognized that radically different alternatives are open to men and women on these questions, and it becomes necessary to find ways to choose among them. Second-order theology was of course always potentially present in the encounter of various first-order theologies with each other, i.e., in every theological argument with an opposing point of view and every missionary encounter with other religious traditions. But it necessarily remained merely potential so long as the opponent's position was not taken seriously as itself possibly the truth. Theological analysis and argumentation was then largely polemics directed toward proving the truth of one's own position and showing the inadequacy of alternatives. One moves to a meta-level only when one realizes the opposing position has perhaps as strong claims to acceptance as one's own, that the different perspectives on life and the world within which men and women live can none of them claim a kind of conclusive truth against the others, that all are visions and imaginative constructions, each with certain appealing features and values as well as some serious deficiencies or shortcomings. In this pluralistic and relativistic consciousness second-order theology first becomes a possibility. The theologian will now be engaged in exploring the character and details of one or more of the great theological schemas known to him or her, attempting to see what functions they perform, seeking to understand what significance or value for human life they may have, trying to grasp why they have been created and whether, or in what respects, they ought to be retained. It becomes important here to find criteria for evaluating theological constructs, for rejecting certain claims and holding to others.

It is at this second-order level—fully conscious of the claims and counterclaims of a variety of alternative positions, aware that all positions, including one's own, are in large part imaginative constructions—that most contemporary theologians, I believe, find themselves. Moreover, it is because we have not been able to move beyond this level—but have, instead, for the most part looked back longingly toward the good old days of first-order theology—that the contemporary scene confronts us largely as a chaos of conflicting claims and counter-claims, with no adequate basis for moving toward any of them with conviction.

What I have maintained in this chapter is that it is now time to move forward from this position and recognize both the possibility and the appropriateness of *third-order theology*. That is, acknowledging that all theological positions are rooted fundamentally in imaginative construction (second-order theology), we must now take control (so far as possible) of our theological activity and attempt deliberately to construct our concepts and images of God and the world; and then we must seek to see human existence in terms of these symbolical constructions. This move presupposes a continuation of the second-order theological work in which most contemporary theologians are already engaged, with its exploration of the utility and significance of various theological concepts and images as well as of alternative theological perspectives and world-views. But it goes beyond that largely analytic and descriptive task to the constructive one of attempting deliberately to formulate theological conceptions and to create theological symbols. Such deliberate constructive activity may be able to develop theological positions to which thoughtful contemporary men and women can give themselves.

The increasing encounter of world cultures, on the one hand, and the development of such sciences as cultural anthropology and the sociology of knowledge and of religion on the other, have produced a level of sophistication which makes first-order theology no longer a viable alternative for many moderns. Second-order theology, however, taken by itself is not adequate to meet the human needs for orientation in life: it leaves us with a chaos of conflicting claims and criteria rather than guidance in the ordering and orienting of our lives. It is necessary for theology now to move to the third-order of deliberate construction if it is to serve contemporary humanity as it has served generations in the past. We must cease looking back with nostalgia to a time when it could be believed that theological concepts and doctrines were rooted in our receptivity to some object(s) over against us, as are the claims of science or common-sense; we must instead develop criteria for guiding and assessing what is frankly our own constructive activity at the heart of theological work; and then we must proceed to the actual work of constructing meaningful theological concepts, images and perspectives. This is the task, both extremely challenging and very frightening, that confronts theology today.

The performance of this task with resoluteness and success may help contemporary men and women bring some greater measure of order and peace into their lives. For they will be enabled once again to see their world, and themselves in that world, as ultimately under a purposeful and humane order. Such a vision can help move us and our world forward toward a more profound humanization.

[1]*Reden über die Religion*. Kritische Ausgabe (Braunschweig: Schwetschke u. Sohn, 1879), p. 128. (A slightly different English translation will be found in John Oman, *On Religion* [New York: Harper Torchbooks, 1958], p. 283.)

[2]An especially clear example of this is to be found in the theology of Karl Barth. Here we are told that "God comes into the picture, the sphere, the field of man's consideration and conception in exactly the same way that objects do.... He is an object on the human plane just like other objects...." (*Church Dogmatics* [Edinburgh: T. & T. Clark, 1936-1962], II, 1, pp. 13-14). It is true of course that Barth recognizes that "although God has genuine objectivity just like all other objects, His objectivity is different from theirs" (*ibid.*), and he devotes considerable effort to working out the distinctions in a subtle and sophisticated way. But the model for thinking about God, with which he is working and which remains despite all qualifications, is clearly that of the perceptual object. In a similar way the philosopher of religion, John Hick, argues that "We become conscious of the existence of other objects in the universe, whether things or persons, either by experiencing them for ourselves or by inferring their existence from evidences within our experience. The awareness of God ...is of the former kind.... while the object of religious knowledge is unique, its basic epistemological pattern is that of all our knowing" (*Faith and Knowledge*, Second Edition [Ithaca, N.Y.: Cornell University Press, 1966], pp. 95, 97). It should not be supposed that thinking about God on the model of the perceptual object is peculiar to writers with a special "objectivist" emphasis. The same model will be found, despite every attempt to avoid it, in Schleiermacher, a man supposedly at Barth's antipodes on this issue. Schleiermacher is unequivocal that "any possibility of God being in any way *given* is entirely excluded, because anything that is outwardly given must be given as an object exposed to our counter-influence, however slight this may be. The transference of the idea of God to any perceptible object, unless one is all the time conscious that it is a piece of purely arbitrary symbolism, is always a corruption...." (*The Christian Faith* [Edinburgh: T. & T. Clark, 1928], p. 18). Nevertheless, when Schleiermacher attempts to explicate the meaning of the term "God," he does so by describing God as the correlative or object of our sense of "absolute dependence," "the *Whence* of our receptive and active existence, as implied in this self-consciousness...." (*ibid.*, p. 16). Clearly, the model once again is the perceivable object, in this case that over against us on which we depend or "hang" (cf. German *Abhängigkeit*). The most recent, and by far the most sophisticated, attempt to found theological work on the "apprehension" of a reality which has quasi-perceptual objectivity will be found in Edward Farley, *Ecclesial Man* (Philadelphia: Fortress Press, 1975). Farley works out a Husserlian doctrine of "appresentation" or indirect apprehension of God through, or along with, direct apprehension of other realities (see esp. pp. 194-231). In many respects his position provides a bridge from the out-and-out objectivist positions of persons like Barth and Hick to that taken in this essay, for Farley clearly recognizes that appresentation has a large component of what I shall call "imaginative construction." However, Farley still attempts to legitimate the theological enterprise by (objectivist) claims about "apprehension" of God, and it is just that vestige of objectivist thinking, I argue here, which theology must once and for all give up.

[3]These peculiarities of the concept of God have not, of course, prevented many believers from speaking of what they called their "experience of God." Since God was thought of on the model of the perceivable object, it was supposed that he could—at least under some circumstances—be directly experienced. Moreover, since he was thought of as *real* in a sense that no created objects are, as transcendent of all finite contingency and relativity, it was natural for believers to identify a profound sense of reality, of presence, of transcendence, as experience of God or the presence of God: "God" was the name most easily called to mind by such special "peak" experiences. What must be recognized here is that referring to such experience as of "God" is already to be operating within a theistic conceptual framework. With the concept of God constructed on the model of the perceivable object, one might expect certain experiences to be in this way identified and interpreted, and such phrases as to "see God" or "experience God" to have a place in the common language. I am holding, however, that close inspection of the concept of God reveals that, whatever it means, it cannot refer in this simple way to an object of direct experience or to anything like such an object, and that to use it in this way leads to serious confusions.

[4]This straightforward referential talk may have derived in part from the presupposition that language consists essentially in "naming," and that behind every noun or concept there must be some "thing" or "object." The tendency to reify concepts has been fairly common in the theological tradition and many of the paradoxes of traditional theology exemplify it. Thus, human nature was often believed to be composed of two (or three) distinguishable "things"— body, soul (and spirit)— and the problem was to understand how these several things could get unified into a single person.

Similarly, christological reflection focused on the question of how the "divine nature" and the "human nature" of Christ—seemingly two distinguishable and almost separable things—could be conceived as unified in one person. And the problem of the Trinity was the issue of how three things—Father, Son and Holy Spirit—were to be thought as one. In these and other theological controversies it seems to be taken for granted that when we have distinct names there must be distinct or separable entities. A great deal of recent philosophical work, particularly associated with the name of Wittgenstein, has shown this sort of move to rest on very gross errors to which we are often brought by the "bewitchment of language." Wittgenstein's basic discussions of these problems are in the *Philosophical Investigations* (Oxford: Blackwell, 1958) and in *The Blue and Brown Books* (Oxford: Blackwell, 1960). In the former there are explicit reflections on Augustine's discussion of the learning of language as typically the learning of names (see pp. 2ff.).

[5]It must be acknowledged that uneasiness about such an undialectical view of the objectivity of God found some expression in Christian thought from the very beginning. Particularly in the so-called negative or apophatic theology it was held that God may not be regarded as any kind of thing or object or essence; indeed, *what* God is is unknowable by us. Here, then, appears to be a complete rejection of objectifying language. However, the matter is not quite that simple. It was not really possible for the negative theology to get away from objectifying talk about God as its actual point of departure: on the one hand, the way of negation gained its meaning by contrast with, or in negation of, the affirmations of the way of eminence; on the other hand, to avoid saying God is unqualifiedly *nothing*, it was still necessary to make some positive statements about God, at least analogically. Obviously there is considerable uneasiness about the use of objectifying models here, but since no other way of understanding language about God was available, those models in fact remained determinative both of affirmations and negations.

[6]In a recent study Karl-Heinz Zur Muehlen shows that it was precisely through radicalizing the received notion of the externality or otherness of God that Luther developed his own unique and powerful position. See *Nos Extra Nos: Luthers Theologie zwischen Mystik und Scholastik* (Tübingen: J. C. B. Mohr, 1972).

[7]Paul Tillich has developed this point in his doctrine of justification even in the most radical doubt (see *The Protestant Era* [Chicago: University of Chicago Press, 1948], pp. xiv-xv).

[8]I cannot consider here the many variations on these themes in the various forms of polytheism. Suffice it to suggest that in a polytheistic scheme some notion of world—or at least of fundamental cosmic order (cf. the Greek *moira*)—superior to the gods seems essential as a unifying backdrop against which the activities of the several gods can be conceived, whereas only in a monotheistic scheme can God be conceived as superordinate to the world and all it contains, indeed, as giving even the world its being and unity.

[9]For discussion of the way in which social and cultural conventions and institutions define a world that is only dimly perceived in consciousness, see Mary Douglas, *Purity and Danger* (New York: Praeger, 1966), and Erving Goffman, *Frame Analysis* (New York: Harper and Row, 1974).

[10]See note 5, above.

3

The Three Moments of Theological Construction

"...man in the last analysis is responsible for the choice of his symbolism."

Robert Bellah[1]

The burden of this essay thus far has been to establish two points. First, that the distinctive and proper business of theology is neither interpretation of the vagaries of religious experience nor exposition of the particularities of scripture or of church doctrine but analysis, interpretation, criticism and reconstruction of the concept and images of *God*, as found in the common language and traditions of the West. All other theological work is logically subsequent to getting clear what we mean by the word "God," however obscure or difficult that task may be. Second, that whatever "God" is finally shown to mean and however true or valid or useful talk about God proves to be, this word does not, and logically cannot, name some reality given directly or immediately in perception or experience but indicates rather a construct of the imagination which helps to tie together, unify and interpret the totality of experience. Theology, thus—talk about God—is essentially a constructive and reconstructive activity, not a descriptive or expository one; and the central problem of theological method is the development of criteria and procedures for carrying on this constructive work.

I cannot in this essay present a full program of such procedures and criteria for theological construction, and certainly I cannot attempt here to present examples of actual constructive theology.[2] The most I can do is open up these methodological questions by making a few tentative suggestions about what is involved in constructing the concept of God, in the hope that others, as they reflect on these issues, will correct, supplement and otherwise modify what I propose. In the past theology has not been clearly recognized as constructive in the radical sense claimed in this essay; and it will take some considerable time, and the work of a good many theological minds, to think through the full implications of this for theological method. I hope, therefore, that my suggestions will stimulate others to reflect on these matters, and that ultimately some relatively systematic and comprehensive statement of theology as construction will be forthcoming.

I

We can begin conveniently by recalling the scope or parameters of the concept of God. As we have noted, it is a very high-level and complex product of the mind's constructive or synthetic powers, for it claims to be related to all other elements and dimensions of experience or reality as the "ultimate point of reference" for all life, action, devotion and reflection. In this respect the concept of God can be compared only with such a concept as "world" (or "universe"). This latter concept, we have seen, does not represent a reality directly given in or to experience, but is instead a regulative idea by means of which we order and hold together the multifarious dimensions of experience in a unified whole; it is, in fact, just the idea of the *whole* of reality.

Although we never directly experience the whole which contains all else (though we may have experiences of vastness, comprehensiveness, "infinity" and the like which are in some way related to the "whole" or suggestive of it, though themselves only a part of it), the idea of the whole is itself rooted in experience. It is based on generalization of the familiar experience of numberless objects each of which is a "whole" made up of "parts." In each of these cases the whole is more than the parts taken simply additively: it is the unified structure of all the parts; it is that which enables us to think this multiplicity as a unity, as one particular thing rather than a mere collection of many things. The concepts of "whole" and "parts" dialectically presuppose and imply each other.

It may be thought that this experientially-derived concept of whole can be, and is, used directly to create the notion of world or universe: the world is the whole, the structured unity of all that is. But that would be an over-simple conclusion. Every experiential whole, though a unity of several parts, is itself simply a part of some larger whole that encompasses it. My hand is a whole made up of fingers and thumb, skin and veins and blood, and so forth (each of which is also a whole composed of parts); but my hand is but a part of the whole that is my body, and my body but a part of the whole self that I am; I, in turn, am part of many communities that go to make up the larger society; and so on indefinitely. "Whole" and "part" are correlative terms, used in diverse contexts to specify many different sorts of relations, but neither is ever an end term of a series. Every empirical whole can be conceived as but a part of some larger whole; every part, so far as it is seen as a unified structure, is itself a whole made up of parts. This means that the notion of world—of the whole which contains all that is, the whole which is not a part of some yet larger whole—is really quite peculiar. Though it is based on the experiential concept of whole, it uses that concept in a way never directly exemplified in experience: the experiential concept of whole, that is to say, serves as a *model* for constructing the concept of world; but the world is not simply one more example of a whole (in the ordinary sense of that word). "World" is a unique notion, a construction of the mind on the basis of experience, but a construction for which there are no direct experiential correlates (a concept without a corresponding percept). This unusual relation to experience does not mean that it is a useless or dispensable or mistaken notion; indeed, it is difficult to see how we could think of ourselves or our experience without conceiving them as falling within some context or whole, i.e., without the concept of world in some sense. But that world itself is never directly perceived or experienced, and for this reason our experience provides only very indirect checks on our concept or picture of the world. A review of the variety of mythologies and metaphysics which humans have produced will reveal how tolerant human experience is of quite diverse, even mutually inconsistent, conceptions of the world.

The concept of world is an important, even an indispensable, notion; but it can be quite misleading. For to have this concept may suggest to us that we know, in some sense, the whole, the structure of all that is. When this happens, the concept has obviously overdetermined our thinking; we never, in fact, know reality as a whole, nor can we clearly conceive what we might mean by that. The whole (the world) is a limiting idea, a forever receding (and approaching) horizon which appears to surround us but which we never can reach. It constantly requires reconception, as new experience and further reflection on experience show earlier conceptions to be inadequate or misleading.[3]

The concept of God functions in part as a corrective of, or check on, the overdetermination of our thinking which the concept of world permits and even encourages. This is because the concept of God relativizes the concept of world thus destroying its absoluteness and finality by holding that the world and all that is in it can be properly understood only by reference to something other than and beyond the world.[4] The relationship between the concepts of God and world is no mere logical one, however, God being understood merely and completely as the (hypothetical) ground of the given world, with nothing more to be said about him than that: such a claim would remain too much within the orbit of the concept of world and would not succeed in relativizing that notion. The metaphors and images in terms of which God has been conceived in Western languages and traditions have therefore implied a good deal more than a merely logically correlative relation. Thus, for example, when God is conceived as "Creator" of the world, the relation between God and the world is not only held to be radically asymmetrical—the world being absolutely dependent upon God for its form, the direction of its development and even its being— but God also is characterized in a definite and particular way. He has a certain independence from the world, has his being in himself and from himself alone, and is in some sense a free agent with respect to the world, who in his free action determines both the being and character of the world. When this concept is employed, it becomes clear that the world is not to be grasped simply in terms of itself, in terms of what is given to our experience and thought; it must be understood in terms of God's "purposes" and "action" which determine and shape it. Thus the concept of the world is no longer the last or ultimate point of reference for understanding life and reality: these—and the world itself as well— can be rightly understood only with reference to the concept of God.[5]

Talk about God (in a monotheistic sense) thus involves imaginative or constructive moves going a considerable distance beyond merely positivistic or descriptive interpretations of what is "given," going, in fact, to what is taken to be the real source or basis of all the givens of perception or experience. Of course, as we have noted, all metaphysical positions (i.e., conceptions of the whole, of the world) involve great imaginative constructiveness; but theistic talk and faith require a double move of the imagination: creation of a conception of the whole, and then of the God who lies behind and is the free and independent ground of that whole.[6]

We are concerned in this chapter with the way in which the fundamental theological notion—God—is built up or constructed because we are interested in gaining some measure of control over that process. We have now isolated two distinguishable moments: the conception of the whole of reality (world), and the conception of the ground of that whole (God) as in a certain way free and independent from the world and thus relativizing it. Though the world can be conceived without also thinking of God (naturalism), it is not logically possible to develop the concept of God without some notion of world. This does not mean, of course, that in a theistic view the concept of God is simply added on to a notion of world which is developed independently, as though just any concept of world would do equally well as any other for theological purposes. On the contrary, the concept of world is decisively qualified when a (monotheistic) notion of God is introduced: the world is no longer conceived as self-sufficient or absolute but is regarded as derivative from and dependent on God. Each of these notions, thus, "God" and "world," comes to interpenetrate and logically determine the other. Formally, the concept of world is logically prior to God, for the latter cannot be developed without the former; but, materially, the concept of God is logically prior to that of world because the way in which the world is conceived is decisively affected by the thought of God as its creator or ground.

This suggests a three-step movement of the imagination which may be conveniently designated the *order of construction*[7] of theological concepts. This movement begins in experience and returns to experience, but in between are major constructive acts of the imagination, the generation of notions of the world and of God. The first step is the imaginative move beyond the items and objects of experience itself to construct a notion of the context within which all experience falls, a concept of the world; the second step is the further constructive leap which limits and relativizes this concept of the world through generation of the concept of God; finally, there is the third imaginative move which returns again to experience and the world, thoroughly reconceiving them now in the light of this concept of God, i.e., grasping them theologically. A movement of this sort seems to underlie the generation of all theological concepts.[8] It was a movement begun implicitly and unconsciously by primal men and women in the original mythopoeic construction of their world, and it was taken over—again largely unconsciously—in the development and refinement of the notions of God and world during the biblical and post-biblical periods. It is a movement which we are now in a position to undertake much more self-consciously and deliberately, and for which, therefore, theologians must now take explicit responsibility. In what follows I shall attempt to analyze briefly each of these three moments of theological construction so as to make clear some of the kinds of choices possible in each. I cannot go beyond that to the development of a full concept or doctrine of God in this essay; but I hope it will be possible to see from this analysis what the major moves in the development of such a concept would be, and what some of the considerations are which must be taken into account in carrying through that task. Above all it is important, if theological work is to become genuinely critical and responsible, that the order of construction be kept clearly in mind as one shapes and refines the theological concepts on which he or she is working. Only in this way will each moment be given its due.

II

The problem of the first moment is the explicit development of a conception of the overall context within which experience falls, a concept of the world. Here is where the attempt is made to articulate the sense or intuition of what is *real*, not illusory or spurious. There are formal and material dimensions of this task. The fundamental metaphor which is formally employed is the one we have been examining, that of the whole. However, that notion taken by itself tells us nothing about what the world is like; it tells us only how the world is related to all the items and dimensions of ordinary experience which make it up. To develop a material conception of the world it is necessary to employ metaphors or models of a more descriptive sort which depict what the world "really is." A number are available and have been employed in metaphysical and mythical construction. The whole may be conceived as nature or being, as essentially power or energy or matter, as mind or will or striving, as mechanism or organism; more mythically, it may be thought of as a cosmic battle between the forces of light and darkness, as an order of fate, as a divine kingdom under a sovereign God. There are of course many other possibilities as well. Each of these images or metaphors sets out a particular understanding of the Reality in which we live and of which we are a part, and it has implications for the way in which the various parts are to be conceived as unified into the whole. Some of the models emphasize more our physical experience as putting us in touch with what is real; others, our moral or religious experience. Some may be so one-sided as to be practically useless in grasping broad areas of experience; others will have surprising flexibility and comprehensiveness.

The attempt to generalize one or more of these models so as to make possible thinking through consistently and coherently a conception of the whole that does justice to all elements and dimensions of experience is the work of metaphysics (cosmology). This is no mere speculative game; it is an attempt to articulate an intuition or understanding of what, finally, is *real*, what is to be taken as the touchstone for understanding life and being and value. It is in and through the metaphysical moment underlying theological construction, therefore, that contact with our sense of what is real and genuine and true is made.

I cannot here spell out procedures for executing the metaphysical task; and few theologians will attempt, or are equipped, to carry it through from foundations to a full superstructure. Exceedingly difficult problems about the nature of experience itself, the relation of experience to fundamental ordering categories on the one hand and to common-sense concepts on the other, the relation of all this to scientific theories and knowledge and to poetic and aesthetic and religious insight, must all be addressed. Instead of directly undertaking this difficult and technical investigation themselves, most theologians either rely on a metaphysical position available to them (e.g., those of Heidegger and Whitehead have been important for many contemporary theologians) or they take over, often too uncritically, interpretations of human life and the world provided by the natural and social sciences, or by tradition or common sense. Contemporary culture in all domains is alive with categories and concepts for grasping various dimensions of experience and the world, and with intuitions and visions of what the structure and meaning of the whole might be. There are the interpretations of the cosmos and its development in contemporary astrophysics, the theories about the fundamental building blocks of matter in modern atomic physics, the conception of life as a complex evolutionary structure which dominates biology; there are the interpretations of self-hood and society developed by modern psychologists and sociologists, and the vast and diverse illuminations of experience and life provided by poets and prophets, artists and novelists. These various concepts and perspectives determine, in many respects, our understanding of the different regions of experience; and they influence, often in hidden ways, our conception of the whole. The task of metaphysics is to make the images and concepts that are determinative here as explicit as possible, so they can be examined and critically assessed, and then to unify and order them into a comprehensive and coherent and convincing conception of the world. Obviously, this is an immense task, extremely difficult and rather speculative.

Theology is involved in such metaphysical criticism and construction because, as I have been arguing, all conceptions of God presuppose notions of the world; a completely articulated theology would thus require a fully developed metaphysics. It cannot be taken for granted that received or common sense notions of the world or the real provide adequate integrating concepts to do justice to all dimensions of experience, or that they provide the appropriate presupposition for the next move which the theologian will need to make, the construction of a concept of God. It is important, therefore, that the theologian give some attention to the metaphors and models he or she is using in conceiving the world. Since theological conceptions come directly in contact with our experience here, with our sense of what is real, this is a point at which the validity of theological work can be in some measure tested. Does the concept of the world being employed in fact do justice to all the multifarious features of experience? Do the operative metaphors and images hang together sufficiently well to bring genuine unity into this vast diversity? Does the concept of the world succeed in articulating what we take to be reality? Above all, can this concept of world be meaningfully relativized and qualified by a concept of God? Only as theologians make explicit their reflection on these matters, affecting the way they conceive the first moment of theological construction, will it be clear to what conception of experience and reality their notion of God is supposed to be relevant.[9] Only thus will we be able to see what "cash value," what actual significance, that notion has.

III

The theologian's proper business is not so much to develop a concept of the world as to construct an adequate concept of God, of that further reality which relativizes and limits the world and all that is in it. However difficult are the problems of metaphysical construction, when we move to theology proper, the issues become even more complex. (This is because, as we have noted, theology unavoidably presupposes cosmology with all its problems and then goes beyond it, adding new ones.) What considerations must be taken into account in working through this second moment of theological construction?

It should be noted first that not all theologians have acknowledged that the concept of God is sharply distinct from the concept of world, as I have emphasized. The notion of God as himself the whole in which "we live and move and have our being" (Acts 17:28), though not prominent in the biblical materials, has appeared from time to time both in mystically oriented writers and also in formal theologians.[10] I wish to argue, however, that since the part/whole metaphor is a principal component in our conceptions of the world, it can only introduce confusion to use it also as a fundamental model for thinking of God. On the one hand, such use suggests two ultimate wholes within which all experience and reality are organized; but that is hardly conceivable. On the other, it suggests that "God" and "world" are not really two distinct realities at all, but rather two different names for, or ways of viewing, the same thing, the context within which human life falls (cf. Spinoza). If this latter is what is intended, it should be explicitly acknowledged. But then one can quite properly be asked to justify his or her use of two such distinctive names which call up quite different images and conceptions. Why are both required? How are they related to each other? How is the actual metaphysical structure, which is designated by these two names, understood? If answers to such questions as these are not forthcoming, surely one of the names should be discarded as misleading and inappropriate. Of the two, it would seem that "God" should be the one to go for, in contrast with the notion of "world, " which is an almost pure example of the use of the part/whole model, "God " (as we shall see) carries quite different connotations and seems to denote a significantly different structure. Thus, use of the part/whole model as the principal basis for conceiving God seems to lead, though this has certainly not always been recognized or intended, toward the dissolution of theology into cosmology.[11] Whatever position one takes on these issues, they ought to be discussed explicitly: if we are to understand what we are doing in theology, we must make clear why it is appropriate or important to introduce the term "God" into our discourse in addition to "world."

I have suggested in this essay that a fundamental reason for introducing talk about God is to relativize and limit the conception of the world. The latter notion always tempts us to hubris, on the one hand, to suppose we know more about the context of our existence than we do, and to idolatry on the other, to regard the structure of reality within which we live and move and which is thus accessible to us as ultimate or final. To introduce the concept of God is to propose an ultimate other than or beyond the world, one who—though he is profound mystery, beyond our ken and not subject to our direct investigation—alone is an appropriate object of our full devotion. Such an emphasis effects a profound relativization of the concept of world: it can no longer be regarded as the last point of reference in terms of which life is to be oriented and understood. (As in the earlier chapters, I am working with a radically monotheistic understanding of God in this chapter.)

Why might one be inclined to move toward construction of such an ultimate relativizing principle? Why not be satisfied with a concept of nature or the world as the ultimate context within which human existence falls? Only if one is aware of certain important values which "God-talk" can provide, and certain serious dangers against which it can help protect, will one feel impelled to move beyond anthropology and cosmology to theology. An awareness of this significant meaning of the word "God" arises out of living and thinking with and in a tradition which in important respects cherishes and attempts to orient itself in terms of "God." Participation in the ritual and life of a church or synagogue, meditation on scripture, growing up in a home where devotion and service to God are taken seriously—all these may open one's consciousness to that profound Mystery beyond all we know and experience in the world, as well as to our constant temptations to idolatrize realities and values found within experience. Or alternatively, a deepening awareness of the special import of the word "God" may emerge as one begins to attend to the role which "God-talk" plays in the great heritage of Western literature, or as one studies religious and theological texts in a college class in the philosophy of religion. But without the awakening of some such interest in that on which the word "God" attempts to focus our attention—and in that sense, without some awareness of who or what God is—the theological enterprise could never get underway. In this respect, then, awareness of God, faith in God, knowledge of God, is the beginning point of properly theological work; and theology may be described as "faith seeking understanding" (Anselm).

Given such an "interest in God" or "awareness of God," how do we proceed to theological construction? Our discussion thus far has emphasized only one important component that must be built into the concept of God: that concept will have to be constructed in such a way as to enable it to relativize the world and all its contents. At first blush this may sound very abstract. But it would be a mistake to suppose that what we are concerned with here is only of intellectual interest and of no significance for "real life": it is the *world* that is relativized and limited by God, everything that is, all finite reality, including, of course, us human beings and all our aspirations and projects, hopes and fears, achievements and failures. A conception of God as the supreme Relativizer is a conception of one who impinges on every feature and dimension of our existence and who thus must be taken into account at every turn. God's "impingement" here is not simply as the fulfiller of our desires and hopes: he is to be conceived as imposing himself so as to restrict and restrain, to cut back and even destroy. To speak of God as the "Relativizer" is to refer in an abstract way to what may be perceived religiously as the terrifying Mystery before whom we can only bow in fear and awe. Nevertheless, this notion does not move us much beyond purely formal features of the concept of God. It specifies the structural relation between the concepts of God and world, enabling us to see more clearly what happens to the concept of world when deliberate theological construction is undertaken; but it does little to fill out the concept of God materially.

The important role of this formal element in the notion of God has long been recognized in the theological tradition. It finds expression in the Book of Job's powerful statement about humanity's littleness and ignorance before God, in the "negative way" of Pseudo-Dionysius, in Thomas' claim that all knowledge of God is at best only analogical. Sometimes this formal element has been concealed in formulas which appear to give a description of what God is, but in fact only state *rules* to guide our theological construction. Thus God has been spoken of as "that than which nothing greater can be conceived" (Anselm) or as "ultimate reality" (Tillich), and it may seem that these phrases define or describe him. In fact, however, neither tells us anything about what or who God is; both are purely formal, expressing rules to guide our theological thinking.

Consider the second phrase first. It instructs us never to stop with any proximate or penultimate reality—anything in the world— regarding that as God. To do so would be idolatry, for God is the ultimate—i.e., the final or last reality, beyond which there is nothing more. But how are we to know when we have reached final reality? The answer can only be that we never do. In the search for God we must always press on, never resting content with what we have discovered or expressed. The real God always transcends and escapes our grasp; whenever we suppose that God has become directly available to us or is in some way (even intellectually) disposable by us, we can be certain it is an idol with which we have to do and not God.[12] Thus the claim that God is "ultimate reality" does not really tell us *what* God is at all; rather it provides us with a rule that we are advised to use in trying to think of him. Similarly with Anselm's famous definition of God as "that than which nothing greater can be conceived."[13] We are instructed here never to regard some reality as God if we can conceive anything as in any way greater. *What* God is, we do not learn from this rule: we learn only that we must test every concept proposed to see whether a "greater" can be conceived.

It is to be noted that both these rules operate comparatively. Who God is, what is meant by speaking of "God," is not given us directly but is grasped only in comparison with something else that God is not: God is not any of the penultimate accessible realities but the final one; God is not any of the realities of which we can conceive something greater, he is that than which nothing greater can be conceived. Our knowledge of God is thus never immediate or direct, never of what he is in himself;[14] it is, in the terms of this essay, something that we imaginatively construct, not something given us in some sort of perception. What shall the "something else" be in relation to which the notion of God is constructed? Obviously, if it is going to be the ultimate or final reality of which we are attempting to speak, that than which nothing greater can be conceived, the "something else" will have to be everything else, i.e., the world. Only in comparison with, and in relation to, the concept of world can the concept of God be rightly constructed. God can be conceived only through setting him over against everything else of which we can speak and know. For only thus will we be able to see that, in comparison with all else, he is the ultimate reality, that than which nothing greater can be conceived.

We have come full circle. My earlier suggestion that the concept of God is the second moment in a move of which the concept of world is the first is now seen to be in conformity with major contentions of the theological tradition; the tradition, however, did not make as explicit and clear as I have attempted to do that theological concepts must be viewed, therefore, as imaginative constructs.[15]

I cannot consider further here the formal features of the relation between the first and second moments of theological construction. We must turn briefly now to the way in which material elements are employed in constructing the concept of God. As we have seen, the formal relation of the second moment to the first tells us nothing about what or who God is. But it is impossible to worship, to order one's life by, or even to think clearly a completely bare and empty "X." God must be conceived in some specific way, as some sort of reality or other, if he is to be conceived at all. How are we to conceive that which we in principle can never perceive? The answer is that the concept of God—like the concept of world—is always constructed with the aid of models drawn from ordinary experience. In accordance with the formal requirement that our idea of God be developed in relation to our notion of the world, the initial move will be, with the help of finite (experienced) relationships as models, to attempt to conceive the (unexperienced but imaginatively constructed) relationship between the world and God. With a bridge from the world to God thus provided, the terms or relata of the finite relationship(s) can then in turn become models for constructing more fully the concepts of God and world.

Such relationships as cause/effect, wholly other/familiar, ground/superstructure, agent/act have been used in this way, with the concept of God developed on the basis of the first term of each of these pairs. Perhaps the predominant material notion that has been used to develop the conception of God is that drawn from the human experience of the creation of artifacts: the relation between God and the world is one of "creation," with God viewed as the "Creator" and the world and all that is in it as his "creature." Once the paradigmatic concept of God in relation to the world has been generated, it becomes possible to elaborate it in many directions with the aid of metaphors drawn from a wide variety of sources. For such elaboration the relational element will no longer need to be central, so concepts and images like light, goodness, mind and being, can be employed. It is essential, of course, if theological construction is to become self-critical and responsible, that criteria for the choice of all such models and metaphors be developed and clearly specified.[16]

One of the most important considerations which must be taken into account when developing such criteria deserves some discussion here. The concept of God plays a much more concrete and existentially significant role in human life than merely relativizing the concept of world. As the ultimate point of reference in terms of which all reality must be understood, God is also the ultimate point of orientation for human existence: it is with reference to God that we can see what significance human life actually has; it is in terms of our understanding of God, and of our relation to God, that we will seek to discern the patterns and forms with which human life should be ordered, how we should live, what we ought to do.[17] This specifically *human* meaning of the concept of God we have not yet explicitly considered, but it is this which most persons have in mind when they speak of him. For God has been seen above all as that reality to which men and women can turn and on which they can rely in face of the ultimate crises and terrors of human life when all other supposed realities have proved infirm and undependable.[18]

Both such anthropomorphic notions as father or king and such highly metaphorical images as light and truth emphasize the great human value or meaning of God. God is one who loves and cares for us like a parent, especially in times of need or crisis; he is our sovereign who maintains order in our world and whom we serve gladly. God is one who overcomes the shadows and terrors which the dark moments of life hold for us by enabling us to see where we are and who we are, and thus to find our way in life; he is one who is completely trustworthy and truthful and who rescues us from the corruptions of error and deceit which threaten to destroy our communal existence. The more metaphysical characterizations which speak of God's unity or power, when taken together with such anthropomorphic and metaphorical notions, underline the profound value and meaning of God for humankind: he is now seen as that ultimate point of reference in terms of which all human life can quite properly be oriented; genuine human fulfillment and meaning can be ours only as we devote ourselves to God. When approached in this way, "God" is seen to designate the ultimate ground for and security of human life, that which is continually working to help "make human life more human" (Paul Lehmann). It is hardly surprising, therefore, that such metaphors as "merciful father" or "powerful savior" were from very early on prominent in talk about God and that they remain among those which are most existentially meaningful to many. It is to be noted, however, that use of such models and images leads toward a conception of God formulated to a considerable extent in terms of human needs and desires.

There is nothing wrong with this in itself. As the ultimate point of reference for all that is, God must also be the focus of orientation for men and women. For that to be possible he must be appropriated as relevant to our deepest human needs and as that which in fact provides fulfillment for our existence. We are living beings driven forward by vital powers within us: unless God has some significant relationship to these actual organic drives and needs, he cannot orient our lives. We are moral beings, living within a fragile communal network of trust and hope and love and loyalty: unless God is in some way himself a moral reality, or at least a sustaining ground for moral existence, we can hardly order our lives with reference to him. We are intellectual beings engaged in the search for truth and aesthetic beings with a deep longing for and appreciation of beauty and harmony and value: unless God also can be conceived as one for whom such matters are of importance, he cannot be the object of our deepest devotion. That is, unless these organic, moral and cultural concerns of ours can in some significant way be attributed also to God, he cannot in fact be the ultimate point of reference which relativizes every aspect of our existence, he cannot be *God* to us. But if he is not God for us—we who are, after all, in the world, "parts" of the world—he is not God at all. In addition to its function of relativizing the world, the concept of God thus has—and must have—a humanized and humanizing quality which the concept of world lacks. God is (quite properly) referred to as "he" (or "she") rather than merely "it."

It is now clear why anthropomorphic images have been so important in conceiving God. The human person is the only reality we know for which moral and intellectual and cultural concerns are of significance. What concrete image could be more appropriate for conceiving God, then, than that of the human being? And how should God's relationship to the world be conceived, if not as the expression of his own intellectual and moral and aesthetic powers and interests? In the notion of God as *Creator* of the world—bringing it into being for his moral and personal concerns, and providentially directing its development and governing its inhabitants so that it, and they, will ultimately reach his moral and personal objectives—these matters have been compactly and economically conceived in the tradition.[19] This notion came to prominence already in the Bible, and it has been the dominant image informing the concept of God in the common culture of the West. It was under the impact of the particular moral character of this Creator-God—especially as that was developed (constructed) by the great prophets and ultimately interpreted in light of the ministry and death of Jesus—that the Western understanding of human morality and self-hood was shaped.

As theology undertakes more deliberate construction of its fundamental concept, it will have to take these facts into account. The fundamental model or "root metaphor" on the basis of which the concept of God is constructed and unified must make intelligible the ascription of moral, intellectual and other humane concerns to him—at least sufficiently to enable God to be the ultimate point of reference for our full human life. This means, however, that the theologian must develop a conception of what is genuinely and authentically human, and fulfilling of the human, as an important prerequisite to and presupposition for constructing an adequate notion of God.[20] In this aspect theology is, as Feuerbach held, a kind of extension of or projection of anthropology; and it is absolutely necessary to get our anthropology clearly in mind if we are to do our theology with sophistication. Doubtless, God must be conceived as ultimately relativizing all our moral and intellectual and aesthetic ideals; but this is not possible unless he is in fact relevant to them: a humanly significant concept of God will thus almost inevitably be in certain respects anthropomorphic.

However, the concept of God, even in its anthropomorphic aspects, is never merely an extension of the empirically human; it is, rather, an idealization or perfection of the human which opens up new possibilities of understanding the human itself. We cannot envision the human as such without thinking of all the limitations—finitude, sin, evil, guilt—under which our life is lived; and thus even the ideally human, when thought of strictly as *human*, is necessarily conceived as very restricted and limited. But when conceived under the guise of the concept of God, the idealization of the human is given license for expansion and development which is virtually unlimited. The empirical reality of humanity no longer prescribes the outer limits of the conception. For this reason, it is in connection with the concept of God that awareness of hidden human capacities and possibilities may first come into view; and only later do they become seen as properly attributable to men and women. Thus, the concept of God, precisely because it was in certain respects an idealization of the human, has made it possible for humanity to stretch and grow in new directions, transforming itself, and its understanding of itself, through history. In this way this concept has functioned as an essential moment in the dynamism of human historical development, and there is no reason to think it may not continue to do so, particularly if it is constructed now with deliberation and care. Mythically expressed: God continually leads us forward toward his perfect kingdom, toward the full realization of our humanity. "Beloved, we are God's children now; it does not yet appear what we shall be, but we know that when he appears we shall be like him" (1 John 3:2).

This close interconnection of the concept of God and the concept of the human obviously introduces certain serious problems. It means that God may be envisioned simply as the one who fulfills our needs or desires, answers our prayers, sanctifies and legitimizes our projects and programs, saves us from tragedy. Often the idea of God has functioned this way, as an ideology legitimating the mundane interests, class structures, or revolutionary movements with which his devotees were concerned; and there seems to be no way of guaranteeing that such misuse will not continue to occur. It should be noted, however, that what I have called the formal element in the concept of God—God's absoluteness, God as the great Relativizer of all things finite—always works against such tendencies idolatrously to identify our wants and programs with God's will. Moreover, the formal element implies that no concept of God—however carefully thought out—may be regarded as adequate: God also relativizes all our attempts to grasp him in concept or image. Thus there is a tension in the concept of God between the motif of absoluteness and the motif of humanization. The motif of absoluteness taken simply by itself is abstract and empty, completely irrelevant to all human concerns except the problem of idolatry; the motif of humanization, however, when overemphasized, produces out and out anthropocentrism and idolatrous ideology. Each of these motifs is necessary to qualify and correct the other in constructing the concept of God, and they always remain in uneasy balance.[21]

The genius of the word "God" is that it unites the relativizing and the humanizing motifs and holds them together in one concept. Thus, that which serves to call into question everything we do and are and experience is at the same time apprehended as ultimately humane and beneficent, that which fulfills and completes our humanity; and that in which we can put our full confidence and trust and to which we can properly give ourselves in devotion is also that which requires a continuous criticism of ourselves, our values and ideas, our activities and customs and institutions. One's relation to God thus combines the demand for restriction and restraint of human hubris and sin with the promise of full humanization and salvation, in a way not matched by other conceptions of what is ultimately real. It is also true, of course, that precisely this combination of the motifs of absoluteness and ultimate human realization or fulfillment is subject to an inversion which results in an extremely dangerous perversion. The empowerment of the human will made possible by confidence that one is doing what God requires can produce terrible uncontrolled fanaticisms that wreak devastation in human affairs. The religious wars, crusades, inquisitions, witch-burnings and intolerance so widespread in Western history are the unhappy evidence of how dangerous the concept of God can be. And the consequent hostility to belief in God, characteristic of the various forms of secularism, atheism and humanism which have appeared in the West, is fully justified in the name of these very motifs of relativization and humanization to which the word "God" itself points.

In traditional theology the guard against misuse of the concept of God in too easy support of one's own position and projects was God's supposed objectivity: what and who God is had been made known in the Bible and especially in Jesus Christ, and we have no right to twist or distort that picture to serve our own ends. The Bible, however, employs many images to speak of God, some not at all consistent with others, and it has been possible, therefore, to invoke the biblical God in justification of some of the most heinous human crimes; indeed, God's blood-thirstiness in certain biblical stories served to legitimate the lowest of human instincts, though other biblical images provided bases for renewal and reform. Thus, the supposed objectivity of God's revelation has hardly succeeded in protecting him—or humanity—from extremely unfortunate subversions. When we realize, however, that all concepts of God are human constructions, we are protected against the destructive heteronomy of the traditional images. But this lays upon theologians new and far-reaching responsibilities. We no longer can settle theological issues by appeal to the authority of scripture or tradition. We must now undertake the much more difficult and hazardous task of deliberately and self-consciously constructing our concept of a God who is an adequate and meaningful object of devotion and center for the orientation of human life. In doing so we are free to entertain on their own merits a variety of models for constructing the concept of God, and to accept or reject them without regard to their scriptural or traditional authorization. We are not free, of course, to use such models simply arbitrarily. As I have been arguing throughout, there are important functions which the concept of God performs; and these must be taken into account in constructing the notion.

To conclude this discussion of the second moment of theological construction, I shall summarize briefly the major considerations to be taken into account in developing a concept of God. First, the formal requirements of the relation of the second moment of theological construction to the first are obviously of central importance; images or metaphors that, when properly qualified, do not meet these formal requirements, may be used only with the greatest caution or not at all. Second, the human significance—the religious power and moral implications—of the model(s) proposed for conceiving God must be carefully examined. Third, logical considerations of consistency and coherence, both within and among the metaphors as used and qualified, and also between the conception of God that results and the conception of the world which orders and unifies all our actual experience, must be thought through carefully. (This matter will be discussed further in connection with the third moment of theological construction.) Fourth, aesthetic considerations—e.g., about the appropriate balancing of metaphors and models over against each other, and about their synthesis into a harmonious and elegant whole which appeals to the human spirit and can attract its affection and devotion—should be taken into account. Fifth and last, the interests, problems and needs of the particular concrete situation within which the theologian is working will have a role to play, since the concept of God must bear relevantly on actual human existence with its particular religious and other commitments. Thus, one might seek to develop a specifically Christian doctrine of God, using certain major creedal definitions, or the figure of Christ, as normative in one's construction; or one might wish to develop a notion of special significance to the poor, or to blacks, or to women, or to middle-class Americans. Giving too much weight to this fifth consideration, however, is somewhat risky and can lead to the presentation of an idol, one who represents merely parochial and partisan interests instead of that than which nothing greater can be conceived.

It is important to remember above all that what is being attempted at the second moment of theological construction is to set out a concept or image of *God*, of that which is finally and above all else *real*. Theology is not a speculative game in which each theologian strives for a more interesting or exotic construct than his or her predecessor; it is the attempt, through hard thinking and imaginative construction, to present the Real with which humans have to do. If a theological construct does not convey a sense of the hardness and firmness of the real, but seems a mere speculative exercise, it fails to be presenting God in any way that he can be acknowledged as the one to be worshipped and served. A God who cannot be grasped as the center of orientation for life is not God at all: such theological construction is a failure. For this reason theological construction cannot stop at moment two, the generation of a concept of God: it must proceed to show how the major dimensions of human life are bound to this God, so that the concept of God does not simply float free as a speculative idea that can be accepted or rejected, but does in fact represent that in terms of which all else—all that we experience as hard and firm reality—must be grasped and understood. Such a reconception of experience and the world in terms of the concept of God, the task of the third moment of theological construction, is indispensable if that concept is to be viable. It is important to recognize that every concept or image of God which we employ is our construct, and it suffers from whatever limitations this implies; but it is our best attempt to construct a conception of what is finally Real, of that in terms of which we can confidently orient our lives.[22]

IV

No one interested in a theistic interpretation of reality would attempt to treat the first two moments of theological construction completely independently of each other, but there is a proper order of construction: the concept of world, as the organization of all our actual experience, coming first, and the concept of God, as a limiting idea relativizing experience and the world, following. If the only ingredient that went into the concept of God were this strictly formal one, there would be little problem in integrating it with the previously developed concept of world; and the notion of an essential third moment of theological construction could be dispensed with. But, as we have seen, the material images and metaphors that give God sufficient concreteness to evoke human devotion and service introduce new and different qualities into the concept. Whether relatively crude anthropomorphisms are used or not, God becomes understood as ultimately beneficient or benevolent to humankind, as a resource who can be depended upon, as the source of all being, goodness and meaning. When filled out thus materially and concretely, it can no longer be taken for granted that the concept of God will cohere easily with the concept of world as previously and independently generated; indeed, it is probable that there will be many tensions. So it is necessary to move on to a third moment of theological construction in which the concept of world is reformulated so as to "fit" intelligibly with the God who is thought to be its ultimate ground and limit.

Simply adjusting each of these concepts to the other, compromising a bit on both sides, is not all that is required here. The concept of God, as the idea of that which limits and relativizes the world, must be given a certain priority, with the concept of world adjusted to and rebuilt on the basis of fundamental requirements which the notion of God imposes. The world is no longer to be conceived simply as the autonomous and self-determining whole of Reality, of which all experienceable and imaginable particulars are parts; the world is now at best the whole of *finite* reality, of creation; and it must be conceived as relativized in all respects, as given its fundamental shape and substance by the ultimate Reality, God, which is to be distinguished from it. So a theistic interpretation or understanding of the world will have to be developed; and appropriate categories, concepts and terms for executing this project will need to be devised. This need not be done simply from scratch, of course, as if the task of reconceiving the world theologically had never been addressed before. Many generations of reflection and construction have produced a whole vocabulary for just this purpose, including, for example, such terms as creation, grace, sin, sacrament, finite being, salvation, contingent event, idol, providence, faith, saint, prophet, miracle. There is, thus, a terminology and a conceptual structure available for assisting in thinking through the relation of God to the world and all it contains.

It would be a mistake to suppose that once the concept of God has been constructed, the concept of the world could be directly and fully derived or deduced from it, and the first moment of theological construction could be ignored or neglected.[23] Such a view would involve a double error. First, it would neglect the fact that the concept of God was itself constructed by a move beginning with the concept of world and thus presupposes that concept; and it would overlook the significance of the fact that all the concrete images and models on the basis of which the concept of God is constructed are drawn from experience in the world; thus, it would fail to take account of the presuppositions and the substance of the concept of God with which it purported to begin. Second, it would fail to acknowledge that we do, after all, have direct experience and knowledge of what is in the world and that our concepts of these matters, and of the world itself, are generated for the express purpose of interpreting and making intelligible to us precisely this experience. It is not possible artificially to deduce or derive from without a whole new theological vocabulary and conceptuality for dealing with our actual experience and thus with the world, and then simply to impose it: to attempt this can only result in abstract and empty talk, talk with no "cash value." If it is experience and the world of which we are attempting to speak, our words will have to be appropriate to and interpretive of what is actually given in and through our experience in the world. It was just this point with which the first moment of theological construction dealt; the concepts and categories generated there, therefore, must be taken very seriously now at the third moment. Whatever is said here, in developing a theistic conception of the world, must do full justice to what was claimed there about the actual qualities and structure of experience.

A major difficulty confronting contemporary theology is the seeming lack of appropriateness or relevance of the traditional theological vocabulary to contemporary experience. In consequence, talk about sin and salvation, sacraments and faith, Christ and the church, often seems to be abstract and empty of meaning, referring to realities and experience in some never-never-land but having little to do with the actual work-a-day world in which we all live. Since it has been precisely these terms and others like them which have provided the connecting link between actual human life and the God who is to be worshipped and obeyed, it is hardly surprising that, with their fading, God also has seemed to grow increasingly distant and irrelevant, and that finally it became possible to announce his complete demise. Clearly we cannot address this problem simply by repeating the same old theological vocabulary, ever louder and more emphatically. That vocabulary was worked out for, and thus was relevant to, the experience in the world had by earlier generations; but it no longer fits well with ours. What is required are fresh attempts to think through and interpret contemporary experience and knowledge theologically. Doubtless, a major resource for this work is the older theological vocabulary, but none of it can be taken over simply because of its importance in the tradition. It can be used only insofar as it does justice to and makes theologically intelligible our experience, as actually grasped and interpreted by us in the language of modern psychology, physics, art and ordinary life. Since it was precisely this experience and these sorts of categories that were utilized in developing the concept of world during the first moment of theological construction, it is clear that that moment will have to be a major ingredient in the third. Only in this way will our notion of God, the product of our second moment of construction, be appropriable as actually relevant to and significant for contemporary life. Only in this way, that is to say, can God become for us an object of genuine worship and devotion, the central point of orientation for our lives and action.

This may seem to be claiming too much, that theological construction can become, in some sense, the basis of renewed faith. When put that way it sounds exaggerated and even blasphemous. But let me turn the claim around. It was because of what earlier generations believed about God, about his faithfulness and love, his care for his creatures and his work in the world, his willingness to send even "his only son" into the world for their salvation, that they were enabled to believe in and trust him. In this sense, as Paul put it, "faith comes from what is heard" (Rom 10:17)—that is, it presupposes having acquired some understanding or knowledge of its putative object. Such prior understanding was made possible for previous generations by the theological tradition, which provided a language and conceptuality that gave a viable and meaningful interpretation of experience. Faith in God has become impossible for many now, not so much because of their stiffnecked sinfulness and rebellion against God as because talk about God—and thus God himself—seems to have little to do with their actual lives. Unless and until this talk can be reconstructed in such a way as to make sense of the major dimensions and problems and projects of contemporary experience, and God can be seen once again to be the God of this world and our God, it is not possible—not *logically* possible, for such an understanding is logically presupposed by faith—to have faith in him. Theological reconstruction is not undertaken simply to satisfy some mere intellectual or speculative impulse; it is a demand of the life of faith itself. In every generation theologians have undertaken to construct and reconstruct the ideas of the world and of God in such a way as to make them intelligible in their time, thus providing this necessary presupposition for life in faith. Theological reconstruction today—now understood as truly activity of construction—is required for the same reasons.

The materials and problems with which theologians must deal in this third moment of theological construction are as wide as contemporary life itself. The work of artists and physicists, social workers and philosophers, historians and economists, urban experts and students of the "third world," spokespersons for the problems of blacks, women and other groups must all be taken into account. Clearly no one person can be master of all this, and different theologians do in fact choose different regions of contemporary life as their special province. But in order to work with effectiveness, the theologian must be alive to many of the main currents and tensions and pressures of contemporary life, together with the principal contemporary (secular) categories for grasping and understanding these matters, for it is precisely this concrete contemporary experience that must be brought into relation with the concept of God.

For this task every theologian needs to find or create some bridge-categories. Among those which have been utilized in recent theology in this way are "ultimate concern" (Tillich), "anxiety" (Kierkegaard, R. Niebuhr, Tillich), "I-Thou" (Buber, Brunner), "existence" (Bultmann, Tillich), "inner history" (H. R. Niebuhr), "secular" (Cox), "hope" (Moltmann). Technical categories developed by persons with no particular theological interest are often susceptible to brilliant theological use and are sometimes so employed, e.g., such Freudian notions as libido, repression and the unconscious; Marxist ideas about the class struggle and the economic basis of all spiritual life; biological concepts like evolution and the interdependence of all life; political slogans like "liberation" or "revolution" or "the free world." There are many concepts available in our culture with which we grasp wide reaches of life in its main currents and tensions, giving us some orientation in the world and some understanding of ourselves. The theologian must collect and sift these concepts, searching for those which will not only enable us to apprehend our experience without falsifying it but will also lend themselves to plausible theological interpretation, i.e., to connection with some of the traditional terms of the theological vocabulary and with the concept of God.

Much current theology is being carried on at what I have called moment three. There is a great deal of attention to the interpretation of contemporary literature and art and to the understanding of urgent social issues such as racism, poverty and problems of the "under-developed" nations. There are attempts to grasp more profoundly the meaning of leisure and play, celebration and imagination, hope and love, emptiness and despair, black experience and female experience; and there is a willingness to look with new openness at quite varied life-styles and to learn from diverse religious traditions. Certainly none of this should be criticized in itself, and much of it should be applauded as absolutely indispensable theological work. Unfortunately, however, the methodological reflection without which such work can hardly be carried off successfully, has seldom preceded or accompanied it. In consequence, it has frequently not been realized that such attempts to deal theologically with contemporary life can be successfully executed only as the third moment of theological construction. When such work is undertaken without careful reflection on the concept of God to which it is seeking to relate a particular domain of contemporary experience, it can hardly accomplish more than bare phenomenological description of that experience, salted, perhaps, with a few *ad hoc* "religious" terms and phrases. This is both bad phenomenology and bad theology, and that for the same reason: the addition of the religious or theological vocabulary to the description and analysis of experience has no clear warrant. It thus serves only to confuse the issue, performing a largely sentimental, rather than substantive, function. Much current "theological writing" is neither very reliable as phenomenological description of experience nor clear in its theological significance or implications because its methodological underpinnings have not been carefully thought through. Methodological self-consciousness is indispensable if theological work at the third moment is to be successful.

This absence of fairly strict attention to methodological considerations in much current writing may not be too difficult to understand. Our experience and understanding and insights seldom follow a logical order like the one I have been describing here. Instead they come to us in complex fits and starts often not clearly related to each other, and it is only in times of reflection that we can sort out logical priorities. Present experience of suffering and deprivation may give rise to hopes and dreams of a new social order and to expectations of new possibilities for human life; and, in their light, convictions about "what God is doing in the world"—and thus new insights into who or what God is—may arise in human hearts and minds. And all this may be put together in powerful "prophetic" sermons or books which persuade many of new and different ways to understand human life and religious experience and symbols. Only later in reflection does it become possible to break these insights and convictions down into the three moments which constitute theological construction, and thus to see what can properly be regarded here as transcription of experience, what is systematic construction, what are new imaginative insights or dreams.

Theological reflection is generated and nurtured by concrete religious life in which such distinctions are only rarely made explicit. That life is carried on largely through the media of ritual, myth (or story) and morality. In ritual and myth intimations of the new humanity and the new world envisioned and hoped for by the religious imagination are portrayed aesthetically as a "virtual world" in which humans are invited to participate. Through taking part in the ritual and "believing" the myth, the faithful begin to open themselves to these new possibilities for their lives; and in moral claims and prescriptions they are called upon to actualize these possibilities, this new life, in their day to day existence. Thus, insight into and understanding of "God" and awareness of the true character and parameters of human existence may well break forth as prophet and poet make claims on human consciousness and conviction quite without regard to the niceties of the "order of theological construction."

For this ongoing movement of creativity in human insight and belief we can only be grateful. But not every insight or perception or conviction, however powerful and persuasive it may initially be, is reliable or true; indeed, many may be false, misleading or corrupting. Theological reflection has the vocation of testing, interpreting and validating all such claims, critically reconstructing them wherever possible into theologically sound formulations, rejecting them when necessary. The analysis of theological claims into three distinct moments of imaginative construction provides us with a schema for this indispensable analysis, evaluative and reconstructive work which is the theologian's central responsibility. This schema enables us to focus directly and explicitly on each ingredient of the theological conceptuality in its own right and in its proper relation to the others.

The first moment of theological construction is the place for pure phenomenological description (so far as that is possible) and for the attempt to put the varieties of contemporary experience together into a concept of the world as a whole. To the extent that one's attention is directed exclusively to the first moment, there is no occasion to introduce theological language (strictly so-called) into one's description and analysis—though it is certainly appropriate to use "religious" language in dealing with "religious experience" or the "religious dimensions" of ordinary experience. The second moment, then, as we have seen, comes as a limiting move on the first and as a positive attempt to set out the human significance of the ultimate reality with which we have to do. It does not consist of phenomenological description at all (except insofar as its models are drawn from ordinary experience) but is, instead, entirely a work of imaginative construction of the concept of God. It is the work accomplished at this moment that provides the foundation and authorization for the introduction of theological terms and concepts at the third moment, the attempt to grasp and interpret experience and the world now no longer simply phenomenologically but theologically. The first two moments, therefore, provide the indispensable grounding for any theological work at the third moment. It is the absence of such explicit grounding in much current theology that is responsible for the confusion, not to say triviality, of much current writing.

I trust it is obvious that these three moments will seldom be taken up in simple serial order as I have discussed them here, even in works on systematic theology. It would be impossible, for example, to construct an idea of God (second moment) without reflecting on the question of whether and how that notion can be conceived in intelligible relation to contemporary experience (third moment): our reflection on the theological interpretation of modern life will affect our formulations of the notion of God, as well as vice versa. On the one hand, such reflection may lead us to ask whether it is any longer possible to think of God as "Creator" of all that is, or as our "Father" (especially in light of what women's liberation theology has already taught us), as Truth-itself or Being-itself. On the other hand, hopes and dreams of new possibilities for human life may give rise to unexpected images or conceptions of God as a search is undertaken for a ground adequate to inaugurate and promote these possibilities. Issues pertinent to the second moment of theological construction thus may well arise out of difficulties or possibilities encountered in the third. Similarly with the first moment. No theologian will develop a concept of the world completely without regard to the fact that he or she intends to develop a concept of God in relation to that concept of world and will ultimately have to furnish a theological interpretation of that same world. In the phenomenological phase of his or her work, therefore, a theologian is likely to have sharper eyes than others for data and patterns susceptible of theological interpretation, and there will be a tendency to highlight these at the expense of others which are more recalcitrant; in the actual construction of a concept of world, the theologian will search for models and images that underline its contingency and the importance of developing a concept of ultimate reality beyond it to relativize and restrict it.

The complexity of theological work requires keeping all three moments of construction in mind at all times so that their dialectical interplay and interdependence can be fully realized and each will be granted its proper integrity. It is at the third moment of theological construction, grounded as it is on moments one and two, that the methodological self-consciousness, which makes it possible to grasp this dialectical differentiation and unity of theological work, appears and can become effective.

V

Throughout this discussion I have taken virtually no account of the fact that most theology has been sectarian in character, Christian or Jewish or Moslem, Protestant or Catholic or Orthodox.[24] This is not because I deny such theologies are any longer appropriate, but rather because I have been trying to isolate and uncover certain features of the basic logical structure of all (monotheistic) talk about God, whether Jewish or Catholic or Methodist. The word "God" is not the private possession of any denomination or religious tradition; it is a common word in English (with cognates in other Western languages), understood and used by virtually all speakers of the language(s). Undoubtedly the meaning and use which this word has come to have has been heavily influenced by what were originally special technical meanings or private connotations peculiar to particular religious communions. Jewish and Christian notions have been especially decisive here; inasmuch as these traditions are the principal source of Western notions of God's singularity and absoluteness and sole right to worship, they have given the concept its core meaning. But since these notions have become a part of the ordinary meaning of the word "God," they are no longer the private possession of these particular communions. It would be more accurate to say, in fact, that today speech about God in church or synagogue presupposes the meaning which the notion has in common discourse, perhaps building upon and qualifying that notion in particular ways but certainly not operating independently of it. The logical structure of this notion of God which is held in common contains, I have argued here, three essential moments; and this structure will be employed in one's theological speech and reflection, whether one's particular standpoint is Jewish, Christian, Moslem or secular. Hence, it needs to be made explicit and taken into account, no matter what sort of theology one takes oneself to be doing.

This does not mean there is no longer any place for, for example, specifically Christian or Jewish theologies. The way in which the concept of God is constructed, the models on which it is based and the emphases that are brought out, will be heavily affected by the religious (or secular) tradition(s) which one finds most illuminating and true. The Christian claim, for example, is that Jesus is the defining model, or at least the ultimate criterion, for understanding who God is ("He is the image of the invisible God," Col. 1:15). For one who regards such a claim as authoritative or true, it is surely proper to construct a doctrine of God accordingly. Such a notion of God will be no less constructed than any other; and if it is a monotheistic notion, it will have to show how Christ transcends and relativizes the world and its contents as well as how the various dimensions of experience are illuminated when understood in relation to him; that is, it will be worked out in terms of precisely the three moments we have examined.[25] Monotheistic conceptions of God constructed on the basis of Torah or Talmud, church dogma or private creed, will each—however various they may be—manifest a similar logical structure. For in each case the intention will be to speak of *God* not some idol, not the world, not anything else at all. So long as there are sharp differences of opinion as to who God is and what he requires of us, it is entirely proper that there be theologians attempting to work out explicitly the grounds for and implications of those diverse views.

The logical structure with which we have been concerned, however, does lay down certain conditions for their work and may be helpful ultimately in assessing their several views. For example, a monotheistic concept of God, I have argued, presupposes a conception of the world and must make intelligible our experience of the world. Insofar as specifically Christian and other conceptions of God do not take the full implications of this seriously in their exposition or interpretation, they must be held deficient or misleading in important ways. Again, every religious communion prefers to think of God in its own terms and of itself as God's "chosen people" whom he favors in various ways above others. So far as the universality of God is thus modified by henotheistic impulses, it is no longer *God* about whom the theologians are speaking but only one of the idols of their particular tribe; and their work is open to the most serious sort of theological criticism.[26] Christian theologians particularly, because of their intense fixation on Christ, have often been guilty of such distortions. To take another sort of example, the concept of God, as we have seen, is constructed in part on the basis of conceptions of what is authentically and properly human. There are obviously vast differences in understanding of the truly human, so this opens up large possibilities for variation in constructing the concept of God. Nevertheless, this component in every theological construct can provide a basis for judging among them. Any view, no matter how authoritatively rooted in some religious tradition, is open to serious criticism if it portrays God as, for instance, morally repugnant and if devotion to him would be dehumanizing.

Thus, sectarian interpretations of God, precisely because they presuppose a logical structure carried in the common language and traditions, are subject to assessment and criticism on the basis of the demands of that logic. It is justifiable to develop a sectarian conception of God only if good reasons can be given for holding that such a view sets forth *God* and not merely some idol from tradition. What I am arguing here is that sectarian theologies can no longer be regarded as autonomous and responsible only to their own private or idiosyncratic norms: they must come before the bar of the gradually emerging common discipline of theology.

What might appear a decisive objection to this position may be made in the name of "divine revelation." The theology I have been discussing here, it might be claimed, is openly human construction. But genuine or true theology is no mere creation of the human imagination: "...we ought not to think that the Deity is...a representation by the art and imagination of man" (Acts 17:29). True theology can only be rooted in God's revelation of himself. It must always be grounded on the authority of what is taken to be divine revelation, whether that be found in scripture or tradition, church dogma or personal conscience. Moreover, whatever has such authority must surely over-rule all criteria developed on the basis of a mere human construct. Since most sectarian theologies are based on what they take to be authoritative revelation, they cannot properly be subjected to the rules or procedures set out in this chapter.

As I have suggested at several points earlier in this essay, this kind of objection rests on a misunderstanding. It neglects the fact that the concept of God is itself presupposed by the idea of divine revelation, that it is precisely this concept, in fact, which provides the ground for claims that the alleged revelation must be regarded as authoritative. In this essay I have tried to show why and how and under what circumstances a concept of God can have this kind of absoluteness and thus can be the basis for such claims. Without a structure of the sort we have uncovered here, a structure that can be grasped only through the mind's powers of imaginative conceptual construction, there could be no reason to regard divine revelation as authoritative. Thus, reference to divine revelation in fact presupposes the sort of logical structure we have been attempting to uncover; it can hardly be used, then, as a basis for rejecting either the claim that our fundamental theological idea is constructed or the analysis of what goes into that construction.

The contention that divine revelation is the ultimate ground of theological knowledge is not, however, entirely misguided. For with certain constructions of the concept of God, specifically those based on the model of the human person or agent, knowledge of God will quite properly be understood as depending upon his act of disclosure: our knowledge of finite personal beings depends heavily on their self-revelatory actions; and knowledge of a God constructed on the basis of such models would also likely be so conceived. Thus, for such a perspective, theological knowledge would have to be understood—whatever the particular human processes involved in producing it—as rooted ultimately in the divine activity of self-disclosure; no other way of understanding the knowledge of God would be consistent with the notion of God as fundamentally active being.[27] This point, however, does not stand in opposition to the claim that our theological ideas, particularly our ideas of God, are constructs of the imagination: it means, rather, that it is precisely through the constructive work of the human imagination that God—ultimate reality understood as active and beneficent, as "gracious"—makes himself known. From this point of view the concept of God itself, in its complex three-moment structure, is to be understood as rooted in and the vehicle of divine revelation.[28] And theological work directed toward explicating that structure more fully, and developing criteria which will make it possible to construct and reconstruct the concept more carefully and responsibly, should be understood as seeking to take God's revelation of himself with maximal seriousness .

---

[1]*Beyond Belief* (New York: Harper and Row, 1970), p. 42.

[2]Examples of some of my efforts to do constructive theology will be found in my *Systematic Theology: a Historicist Perspective* (New York: Scribners, 1968) and in *God the Problem* (Cambridge, MA: Harvard University Press, 1972). My understanding of theology as primarily constructive activity grew up in the context of, and in reflection upon, what was going on in this and subsequent theological writing. However, for just that reason none of these materials exemplify a full and explicit application of the methodological ideas presented in this essay. Those ideas were still somewhat inchoate and undeveloped—though clearly implicit—in most of that writing.

[3]Proper phenomenological description of the context within which we live and act will require horizon-talk as well as whole-talk. The concept of the horizon probably expresses primitive human experience more accurately than that of the whole, the concept of world better representing more highly-structured experience. Our primitive experience is not so much of "being-in-the-world" as it is something like "being-in-a-setting" or "being-in-surroundings." The notion of "world" is too definite and complete, too well-ordered, to be used here. It involves the idea of a structured or ordered whole of which we are a part; but this primitive experience is not of such a whole at all, but rather of being located at a point with indefinite horizons circumscribing us in all directions. However, as we begin to discern order in life and experience and begin to become aware of ourselves as at the center of this order, we find it useful—even necessary—to construct concepts of self and world and to interpret experience in terms of these more structured notions. Experience then becomes apprehended by us as falling within the world, not simply as bounded by an indefinite ever-receding horizon. This idea of the world as a determinate and ordered whole may all-too-easily become frozen and fixed. The phenomenologists are right, therefore, in introducing the concept of horizon as a qualification or corrective making possible more accurate phenomenological description of certain features of experience. But the more determinate concept of world has its part to play as well, and it is particularly in relation to this concept (rather than "horizon") that the notion of "God" can be understood. As we shall see in what follows, the idea of God functions conceptually with reference to the world somewhat as horizon-talk functions phenomenologically.

[4]One could argue that all forms of naturalism and positivism sit too comfortably with the finality or ultimacy of the concept of world, giving too much play to its tendency to overdetermine our thinking.

[5]If I were going to develop the concept of God as Creator here, it would be necessary, of course, to qualify and modify these rather general statements in a number of important respects. It is not my intention to present a theologically refined doctrine of creation, however; but rather simply to call attention to the way in which the concept of world is affected and relativized by the notion of God as its Creator. For a more elaborate treatment of the doctrine of creation, see my *Systematic Theology*, esp. chs. 9, 18–20.

[6]The complexity of this double move may be what lies behind the talk about experiences of "depth" (Tillich) or "ultimacy" (e.g., Langdon Gilkey, *Naming the Whirlwind* [Indianapolis: Bobbs-Merrill, 1969], esp. Pt. II, chs. 2–4), by some of those who claim theology is founded on "religious experience(s)." Even as described by these writers, however, it is not apparent that either ultimacy or depth are directly experienced as such. Both notions are, in fact, based on models drawn from ordinary experience and with no obvious religious implications at all. "Ultimacy" is drawn from a model based on the temporal order and referring to "lastness" or "finality"; "depth" is a spatial notion which employs the idea of three-dimensionality as over against a flat surface. Both of these models or images thus suggest a sense of something more than the given, something away from or "beyond" the given, a notion of "transcendence" (note again the spatial models employed in the last two characterizations). It is of course possible—and highly suggestive—to apply models of this sort to experience, especially those experiences (or dimensions of experience) which are somewhat murky or unclear or ambiguous, and thus susceptible to a variety of interpretations. The application of such metaphors opens the experience to religious or theological interpretations. But this is because the experience is being interpreted in terms of these models or images (which may or may not be accepted by other phenomenologists as appropriate), not because "ultimacy" or "depth" are directly read off the (supposedly "raw") experience itself. Since the concept of God involves complex imaginative moves beyond the directly experienced order, as we have seen, it is not difficult to understand why such terms as these might be given a significant religious or theological use. But the justification for that use is to be found more in this structure of the idea of God, than in the simple occurrence of certain highly ambiguous experiences.

[7]The order of construction, it may be observed, is not to be confused with either the so-called order of being or the order of knowing, or, for that matter, with the temporal order of the development of theological concepts in either human history as a whole or the individual.

[8]I should perhaps note here that, although this "cosmological" way of understanding how the idea of God is generated is the most convincing to me, I do not mean to be claiming it is the only possible alternative; other analyses, e.g., more "existential" ones, are also possible (see note 18, below); and it is important that their plausibility be explored, though that cannot be undertaken here. One value of the conception of theology as construction is that it opens up for us the possibility of examining how alternative conceptions of God have been put together, so that we can better judge their adequacy.

[9]The somewhat slipshod practice of many theologians with respect to developing a satisfactory concept of world has resulted in incongruities and inconsistencies. Thus, though the conception of the world as fundamentally *matter* has often been claimed (perhaps mistakenly) to be theologically unsatisfactory, it has been supposed that concepts like *nature* or *being* pose no serious problems. I cannot discuss any of these assumptions here, but some of the theological difficulties with the notion of "nature" as a unifying metaphor for conceiving the whole have been pointed out in "A Problem for Theology: the Concept of Nature" (*Harvard Theological Review* [1972] 65:337–66) and some comments on difficulties with the concept of "being" will be found in ch. 4 of *God the Problem*.

[10]This usage is rather widely employed (often uncritically) in contemporary theological writing. Consider especially the "panentheism" of Charles Hartshorne and his followers (see, e.g., *Reality as Social Process* [Glencoe, IL: The Free Press, 1953], ch. 6; and [with W. L. Reese] *Philosophers Speak of* God [Chicago: University of Chicago Press, 1953], "Introduction"). Paul Tillich's doctrine that God is "being-itself" (*Systematic Theology I* [Chicago: University of Chicago Press, 1951], pp. 235–39) also makes it difficult to draw a sharp line between God and the world; his use of other metaphors, however—"ground of being," "power of being"—suggests such a distinction. A major difficulty with Tillich's theology is that the mixture of metaphors is such that it is very hard to get clear just exactly what he is trying to say about God.

[11]Cf. Paul Tillich: *"... deus sive natura* [is] a phrase which indicates that the name 'God' does not add anything to what is already involved in the name 'nature.'" *(Systematic Theology* I, p. 262.)

[12]I have developed this idea briefly through a distinction between the "real God" and the "available God" in *God the Problem,* ch. 5.

[13]*Proslogium,* ch. 2.

[14]This of course accords with Thomas' contention that we (in this life) cannot know God in his essence or nature but only in his relations to us *(Summa Theologica,* I, 1, Q. 12, arts. 11–13).

[15]The so-called cosmological argument for the existence of God provides a good example of this deficiency. This argument is based upon the recognition that in the order of construction of theological ideas the concept of God comes second after, and is dependent upon, the concept of world; on the basis of this insight, God's existence is to be proved. The argument would be valid only if the concept of world drove us on necessarily and unavoidably to a concept of God, e.g., if "contingency" were necessarily seen as an essential characteristic of the world. But contingency is recognized as a mark of the world only when the latter is seen as not self-subsistent but as "creation," i.e., when it is grasped as dependent upon something beyond itself, dependent upon God. Such a conception of the world belongs properly to the third moment of theological construction not the first: it can be developed only after, and in dependence upon, the concept of God. The cosmological argument is not persuasive because it holds that the contingency of the world is directly given. The proponents of the argument were correct in seeing that the concept of world logically precedes that of God in certain respects, but they were mistaken in not realizing that the movement from the concept of world to the concept of God is a free act of imaginative construction and is not logically necessary.

[16]Models with quite various implications for the conception of God have been employed in the tradition. Some are highly anthropomorphic, e.g., father, lord or king, judge, husband; others, more abstract, e.g., First Cause, Substance, Ground, Power, Being, the One; still others, highly metaphorical, e.g., light, truth, love, Most High. It is not possible here either to list all the models which have been used or to classify or assess their relative appropriateness. Obviously it is important that comprehensive catalogs of such metaphors and models be developed along with criteria for evaluating their theological usefulness.

[17]In the light of this function of God, as providing fundamental orientation in human life and action, we can see from another side why it is important not to confuse the concept of the world, based on the model of the "whole," with the concept of God. The Whole as such can provide no principles for discrimination or evaluation of particular objects; it could, thus, provide no criteria on the basis of which persons could make effective and responsible decisions about potential courses of action. The Whole cannot provide orientation for an acting being that must make particular choices and work toward specific objectives, a being who is in the process of creating and shaping itself in and through its very actions. For this reason it becomes a source of confusion when this metaphor is utilized as a principal basis for constructing the concept of God, that reality which is to provide us with fundamental orientation in life.

[18]It might be argued that the "cosmological" sort of analysis of the concept of God that I have presented—which emphasizes God's relationship to the world—is highly misleading, for the real function of images and concepts of God is to enable us to focus consciousness on that object of devotion which renders human life meaningful in the face of devastating crises, i.e., which brings salvation. For such "existentialist" interpretations of the idea of God, our "worldly" experience may be regarded as of no signifi-cance—or perhaps exclusively of negative significance—for understanding who or what God is (cf. Bultmann and the early Barth). Rather, the significant correlation is "God and the soul" (Augustine). By "God" we mean that ultimate Spirit which is the ground and goal of our finite human spirits; and the question of the "world," and of our ordinary experience in it, is thus fundamentally irrelevant for theology. It is obvious that a construction of the idea of God along these lines will move quite differently than has the argument of the present chapter—e.g., the first moment would be an analysis or interpretation of the self or of human existence; and, on the basis of this, the second moment, God, would have to be constructed. My reasons for not going this way should not be difficult to discern from the text, so I will not make them explicit here. I mention this alternative understanding of the concept of God here to reinforce my claim that in moving now to what I shall call the "humanizing" motif of the concept of God, we are still dealing with what is central and indispensable; indeed, this motif is so significant in Western traditions that some writers of existentialist persuasion have taken it to be exhaustive of the concept. Whether the more "existentialist" or more "cosmological" understanding of God is correct is a matter not to be decided in this essay; that is properly dealt with when one attempts actually to construct a notion of God. It

should be evident that although I find the cosmological approach more convincing, and have therefore used it as my example in trying to show what is involved in theological construction, the conception of theology as construction does not itself depend on the notion that the idea of God is built up partly on the basis of the idea of the world. It is a virtue of the methodological approach being developed in this essay that it facilitates isolating and grasping the real significance of such fundamental theological issues as these, thus making it possible for theologians to choose deliberately and responsibly from among them.

19The image of Creator has the advantage of underlining God's autonomy and freedom in a way that almost no other model or concept could. Metaphors like "power" or "energy" represent realities that can affect us in various decisive ways; but we can also turn these (impersonal) realities to our own uses (e.g., electricity, light, heat); we simply need to learn the laws by which they operate. Such power is not really *autonomous* but is a manifestation of an order or law which can be studied and in some measure controlled by men and women. The one model of genuine autonomy or self-determination is the human self. In the self's cultural creativity and moral responsibility, we have an image of what genuine freedom or self-determination might be: an action from within which produces that which has never been before (creativity), an action which is taken deliberately and with conscious regard of its consequences for other beings in the field of action (moral responsibility). No other model performs as well the essential purpose of exemplifying God's genuine autonomy and independence and freedom, his aseity; its widespread use should therefore not be surprising. Moreover, this model is able to accommodate both the relativizing and the humanizing motifs in the concept of God, and it thus facilitates constructing that concept in such a way as to call forth human worship and service. Precisely these strengths are also its weaknesses: it lends itself all too easily to excessive anthropomorphism and objectification; and if it is not understood to be a human construction, it may thus foster a naive idolatrous faith.

20It is at this point, perhaps, that christology has played its most significant role in theology in the past, and it is here that it can probably still be of central importance. Jesus' emphasis on God's fatherliness, forgiveness and love, taken together with the example of his own ministry and the selfless sacrifice in his death, provided an image for the early Christians both of the kind of being God was and of the kind they should be. As one who represented for them "true humanity" he served as the basis for a reconception of what "true divinity" was. It was just this coincidence of the human and the divine in Jesus that was stressed in the claims that he was God's unique "son" or "word," that he was "divine" as well as "human" (see my *Systematic Theology*, chs. 11–14, for further discussion). Many will hold that Jesus still represents more adequately than any other figure, or any mere concept, that which is truly and authentically human. For all who take such a position theological construction will continue to require a strong christocentric emphasis.

21Some might wish to deny—on the basis of an analysis of the concept of God as it has developed in the West, or by reference to some supposed revealed notion of who God is—my suggestion that the monotheistic concept of God is composed essentially of the two motifs of relativizer and humanizer. Alternative analyses will surely be forthcoming, and I welcome them; it is only through discussion of such fundamental issues that the theological enterprise can be advanced. Some, while granting that these motifs properly characterize the received concept of God, may nevertheless wish to move down different lines in their theological construction. This, too, is certainly legitimate, so long as good reasons are given for making the new moves and a plausible argument is given for holding that they are properly *theological*, i.e., that they deal with "God. "

22Some might wish to treat this emphasis on the "hard reality" which must characterize a concept of God as a third motif which must be taken into account alongside the motifs of absoluteness and humanization; certainly it is this sense of the "hard reality" of the world we live in which will often restrict most decisively the anthropomorphizing tendency to see God as overly "humane" or "kindly." This approach might also provide a way to introduce more directly "experiential" materials into the construction of the concept. I think an argument could be made for such an alternative. However, I have not taken it myself because (as I have argued in the text) it seems to me incorrect to suppose that God is ever, or in any respect, directly experienced. I think the stress on the reality of what we are dealing with when speaking of God properly belongs to the first motif I have isolated—God as the ultimate point of reference in terms of which all else must be understood, God as the ultimate Relativizer of everything finite—and the sense of the *experienced* real belongs to the first and third moments of theological construction, not the second.

23To have attempted something of this sort was the fundamental error of the most powerful theological construction of this century, that of Karl Barth.

[24]I have deliberately not widened these characterizations further here, suggesting the possibility of, e.g., Hindu or Buddhist theologies. This is not because I wish to deny that possibility, for it certainly warrants careful investigation. It is, rather, because the concept of God with which we have been concerned (in contrast with concepts of gods, or powers, or fate, or certain other conceptions of what is "ultimate") is a largely Western notion, developed in the cultures heavily influenced by the three descendants of ancient Israel: Judaism, Islam and especially Christianity. I have argued throughout this essay that it is, and always has been, the task of theology as a discipline to deal with this peculiar concept; and I have tried here to throw light on what is involved in doing just that. The relation of this concept to other important notions of what is ultimate is of course a very significant problem also, one that is logically interdependent with the problem addressed in this essay: we cannot get fully clear what we mean when we say "God"—how this notion functions in thought and experience, just what its possibilities are as well as the difficulties in using it—without seeing it in comparison with other conceptions that perform similar functions. I hope, therefore, that studies comparing major religious and cultural traditions will continue to move forward rapidly. Such studies, however, presuppose some genuine understanding of major claims and concepts stressed in each of those traditions just as truly as they are needed to help further such understanding. The present essay—and theology generally, I hold—is an attempt to make a contribution toward such understanding of the central Western religious symbol.

[25]In the Christian tradition this essential relationship of Christ to transcendence on the one hand and to the totality of experience in the world on the other has long been emphasized, and the doctrine of the trinity is an attempt to work out certain aspects of this problem metaphysically. (It should be noted, however, that my three "moments" do not correspond exactly to the three persons of the trinity and are not derived from that doctrine.)

[26]For critical discussion of such theological "henotheism," see H. Richard Niebuhr, *Radical Monotheism and Western Culture* (New York: Harper & Row, 1960).

[27]I have attempted to work out some of these issues in more detail in my *Systematic Theology* and in *God the Problem*. In the latter see esp. chs. 4 and 7.

[28]Cf. Karl Barth on Anselm's generation of his famous concept of God: "*Quo maius cogitari nequit* only appears to be a concept that he formed for himself; it is in fact as far as he is concerned a revealed Name of God." (*Anselm: Fides Quaerens Intellectum* [London: SCM Press, 1960], p. 77.)

EPILOGUE:
Theological Construction and the Question of Truth

The question of whether theological claims are *true*, and if so in what respects, has not been straight-forwardly addressed in this essay. This is because this question, as usually understood, presupposes what I have called the "perceptual model" of reality, where the correspondence of our ideas with the reals "out there" is a proper issue. It is appropriate to raise the question of truth in this form with regard to every object or quality in the world, for here we are concerned with the way in which one item in our conceptual scheme relates to and represents one item in what we call (also in our conceptual scheme) experience or the world. But where it is the *world-itself* we are trying to conceive, the whole within which everything else falls—including not only all facts but also all our symbols—there is nothing outside our conception against which we can place it to see whether it "corresponds": just as every thing is within the world, so also everything must be conceived as included within the conception of the world. With this conception, then, criteria of correspondence cannot be applied: only criteria of coherence and pragmatic usefulness to human life are relevant and applicable. If these considerations hold for the concept of world, how much more must they apply to the concept of God, built up as it is through even more elaborate imaginative constructive moves.

We can scarcely avoid being interested, of course, in the question whether our ideas of world and God are valid or true, i.e., how well they represent what is the case. However, since these ideas are imaginative constructs not directly grounded on perceptual receptivity, the usual way of checking this matter is not open to us. Only indirect checks are possible. For example, how well does our concept of the world enable us to deal with every dimension of experience and to act fittingly and with a minimum of false steps in life? To what extent can our concept of God in fact function as an ultimate point of reference for all our experience and action? for our concept of the world? for our human aspirations and ideals? In how far does it help sustain and realize our full and authentic human potentialities? The most a theologian can do is attempt to show that the interpretation of the facts of experience and life, which he or she has set forth, holds within it greater likelihood than any other for opening up the future into which humankind is moving—making available new possibilities, raising new hopes, enabling men and women to move to new levels of humanness and humaneness, instead of closing off options and restricting or inhibiting growth into a fuller humanity. The theologian can attempt to show that a theistic way of grasping the world is requisite if human life is to be enhanced, that other perspectives threaten life with deterioration, destruction or at least a kind of stasis in our present unsatisfactory condition.

On the comprehensive level with which theological concepts deal, the appeal—after internal coherence has been assured—can ultimately be only to pragmatic considerations of this sort. And the verification of theological claims will be found in the degree to which individuals and communities—as they attempt to order their existence "under God"— actually find new life, genuine fulfillment, their own humanity (i.e., what has traditionally been called "salvation"). It should not be forgotten, of course, that advocates of alternative conceptions of human life and the world have no advantage in this respect: all human concepts of reality or the world are constructs which have significance for us to the degree that they provide us with useful maps for dealing with life; none can be checked in some extra-pragmatic way to see whether they "correspond" to "reality."[1] If we realize what is involved in such all-comprehensive concepts, we will not expect more.

Thus a theological construct may be regarded as true—in the only sense of "true" properly applicable here—if it in fact leads to fruitful life, in the broadest and fullest and most comprehensive sense possible. We can never jump out of our concept of the world, or of God, in order to see if the "real world" and the "real God" correspond to those concepts; we have no independent source of information about them which can provide a check on these ideas. The only test we can apply is to see how satisfactorily they do the intellectual and cultural work for which they have been constructed.

The criteria for assessing theological claims turn out in the last analysis, thus, to be pragmatic and humanistic. This is not because theologians are necessarily committed to pragmatic or utilitarian conceptions of truth in general but rather because such considerations—when understood in the broadest possible sense—are the only ones by which a way of life, a world-view, a perspective on the totality of things, a concept of God, may ultimately be assessed.

---

[1]For further discussion of these issues see Nicholas Rescher's two books, *Conceptual Idealism* (Oxford: Blackwell, 1973), esp. ch. 9, and *The Primacy of Practice* (Oxford: Blackwell, 1973). See also my article, "Metaphysics and Theology," *Cross Currents* (1978) 28:325-341.

Appendix:
The Three Moments of Theological Construction

The exposition of the "three moments of theological construction" in the text of *An Essay on Theological Method* may easily give a misleading impression. Despite denials in the text (pp. 77–78), it seems to be suggested that there is a certain proper serial order in which one might—or possibly should—proceed in one's theological work. One should begin, it seems to be suggested, by working out a conception of the world; then a conception of God; then a conception of God and world in relationship. But in actuality no one does, or could, proceed this way. Theology always in fact begins with someone's consciousness of God's relationship to or significance for the world; it is an attempt to make more explicit what is implicit or unclear in that consciousness. (Theology is in this sense "faith seeking understanding." Cf. pp. xx, 61.) It is only because the theologian thinks of God as in some way significant for, powerful in, or relevant to contemporary human life, that he or she has an interest in the theological task at all. At the same time, however, it is because the theologian is aware of, or senses that, this relationship of God and human existence is conceived wrongly or inadequately, or in such a way as to have unfortunate consequences in life, that theological reflection and reconstruction are perceived as important tasks to be undertaken. Thus, the beginning point of theological reflection and work is some awareness of the meaning or significance of God, on the one hand, and some consciousness of the inadequacy with which God is grasped or understood or expressed, on the other. This kind of double-consciousness could appear only where God and world are thought together or in relation to each other. But in the text that sort of interconnection is said properly to occur only at the third moment of theological construction. It might seem, then, paradoxically, that theological reflection must begin at the third moment, not the first.

This inference would be quite misleading, for the third moment is intended to represent the completion or synthesis to which one comes as a result of one's theological work, not the starting-point. How, then, are these issues to be understood? What is missing from the text is any attempt to describe the *psychological order* through which constructive activity moves; the doctrine of the three moments deals with essentially logical not psychological issues. In order to understand the order of construction more psychologically it is necessary to posit a "Moment Zero" which precedes moments one, two, and three as discussed in the text. The consciousness underlying and initiating theological reflection, analysis and construction occurs at Moment Zero, the concrete situation of the believing/unbelieving/puzzling theologian. The theologian may be white or black, male or female, American or African or Indian, pious or skeptical, straight or gay, bourgeois or revolutionary—and of course there are many other concrete determinations or biases that might be in significant ways determinative of the theologian's awareness and understanding. These are not necessarily disadvantages or serious limitations; they express, rather, the actuality and concreteness of the experience and the world known to the theologian, and thus the access to life and reality available to her or him. But they also mean that the understanding of God and humanity and the world with which the theologian begins will be relative and limited in certain significant respects.

The doctrine of the three moments of theological construction is an attempt, now, to articulate the moves which must be made in order to deal with the "dissatisfaction" (at Moment Zero) that gives rise to theological reflection. It is an attempt to show how the understanding of God and human existence and their relationship at Moment Zero can be taken apart and reconstructed from the ground up into a more adequate view.

The doctrine claims that (1) implicit in all talk about God and humanity, or God and the world, is a *conception of the world*, i.e. a conception of the totality of human life and the overall context within which all human life falls. It is important to note that it is *the* world, not simply *my* world, which is presupposed here. The word "God" does not refer simply to the reference point for my experience or my group: it intends to indicate the "ultimate point of reference" for all that is. This requires us, then, consciously and explicitly to build into our thinking about God a notion of "all that is"; this is what the concern with "the world," at the first moment of theological construction, is all about. The relatively parochial and narrow character of our initial theological understanding—proceeding as it does out of our concrete experience and concrete situation—can be to some extent overcome if we attempt to make as explicit and straightforward as possible the notion of "the world" which is presupposed in our concept of God. Thus, the first moment of theological construction constrains us to widen the boundaries of our ordinary thinking from beyond the circle of our own experience, or the experience of our group, to a notion that includes the experience of others different from ourselves, indeed, makes place for "all possible experience." This, of course, does not involve a repudiation of one's own concreteness and relativity; it requires, rather, that one try imaginatively to set these in a wider context. The God we worship and with which we are concerned is not simply "our" God but the God of "all that is," and if we are to think clearly of God and God's relation to us this must be built into our notion. It is the work of the first moment of theological construction to attend to this set of issues.

But (2) God is not to be identified with the world: God is the ultimate point of reference which relativizes the world and humanizes it. So an imaginative leap from the first to the second moment of theological construction is required in order to develop an explicit doctrine of God. This second moment draws on the universalization attempted at the first moment, and in addition it draws on models and conceptions of humaneness, thus giving God a "humanizing" character. Much of this additional material, of course, will be drawn out of the Moment Zero with which the theologian begins. That is, the consciousness of God, of the human and the humane, of injustice and oppression and alienation and evil which the theologian has experienced in his or her concrete existence will provide much of the material with which she or he works. But these now will be refined and criticized in light of the explicit attention to the various alternative models for conceiving God available in the tradition or otherwise known to the theologian. So at the second moment the central task of theological construction is addressed: the attempt to formulate explicitly who or what God is.

(3) Having done this, it becomes possible to return to the question of God's relation to the world—the question with which theological

reflection began at Moment Zero—and to work that out now explicitly in terms of the (criticized and more purified) doctrine of God, as well as the more adequate understanding of the world developed at the first and second moments. Here again, of course, the theologian's experience and world in all their specificity and concreteness may well be expressed and interpreted—as at Moment Zero—but these will now be placed in a wider and more universal context of understanding, and the conception of God to which they are linked will be expanded significantly beyond its original parochialness and relativity. Thus, the activity of the theologian will come to its (temporary) completion or resting place with God seen once again in significant relationship to concrete human life and the world. It is important to note that this is not simply a return to the original Moment Zero, however. Theological work as described here moves in a spiral, not a circle, and if it has been carried through with some measure of success, the theologian will have come to a new and theologically more sophisticated understanding of the elements making up her or his religious consciousness.

The arrival at Moment Three, of course, does not mean that theological activity comes to an end. To the extent that the new formulations and the new consciousness remain unsatisfactory, or, with respect to new sorts of difficulty that arise, the stage is set for further reflection, analysis and construction. So the new Moment Three will become the Moment Zero for another round of the theological task.

G.D.K.
12/18/79